# Touched By The Fire

D1446607

Luke and Acts

from

THE NEW TESTAMENT
in Today's English Version

Third Edition

Published for
**KEY 73**
by the
AMERICAN BIBLE SOCIETY

*This portion of Holy Scripture is a part of the New Testament of our Lord Jesus Christ. We urge you next to read the entire New Testament, which may be secured from your church, religious bookstore or the American Bible Society.*

© American Bible Society 1966, 1971

ENG. PORT. LUKE and ACTS TEV 460P
ABS-1973-800,000-1,300,000-A-2

Printed in U.S.A.

# PREFACE

Luke's account of the Good News is a brilliant description and defense of Christianity—the new way of life so much misunderstood by the sophisticated and often cynical Greco-Roman world. A physician by profession and a qualified historian as demonstrated by his careful study of the evidence, Luke sets forth in considerable detail the significant events of the life of the world's most extraordinary person, Jesus Christ, Son of Man and Son of God. Luke includes a number of well-known parables not reported in the other Gospels: the Good Samaritan (10.29-37), the Prodigal Son (15.11-32), the Rich Man and Lazarus (16.19-31), and the Pharisee and the Tax Collector (18.9-14). Luke is particularly concerned with the universal nature of the gospel, as a light for revelation to the Gentiles and as God's salvation for all mankind.

The Acts of the Apostles is the second volume of Luke's history and defense of early Christianity. This story is told in terms of an ever wider ministry, directed by the Spirit of God to more and more people: Jews, Samaritans, an Ethiopian official, a Roman army officer, the people of Asia Minor, Greece, and finally Rome. Thus the Christian faith, which had begun as a Jewish movement, soon became largely Gentile.

More than one-half of Acts (from chapter 13 to the end) is concerned with the intensive missionary efforts of Paul, whose extensive travels, constant teaching, devoted care for the believers, and profound insights concerning Christ's death and resurrection influenced so greatly the character and development of the Church. Luke, as the "beloved physician," accompanied Paul during some of his later travels (10.16), and was thus in a particularly strategic position to interpret the real significance of the Christian Way—so despised and misunderstood by the pagan powers of ancient times.

This translation of the Gospel of Luke and the Acts of the Apostles in Today's English Version has been prepared by the American Bible Society for people who speak English either as their mother tongue or as an acquired language. As a distinctly new translation it does not conform to traditional vocabulary or style, but seeks to express the meaning of the Greek text in words and forms accepted as standard by people everywhere who employ English as a means of communication. Today's English Version of the New Testament attempts to follow, in this century, the example set by the authors of the New Testament books who, for the most part, wrote in the standard, or common, form of the Greek language used throughout the Roman Empire. As much as possible, words and forms of English not in current use have been avoided; but no rigid limit has been set to the vocabulary employed.

The text from which this translation was made is the Greek New Testament prepared by an international committee of New Testament scholars and published by the United Bible Societies. Verses marked with brackets [ ] are not in the oldest and best manuscripts of the New Testament.

The basic draft of this translation was prepared by Dr. Robert G. Bratcher. It was submitted to a panel of specialists for study and finally reviewed and approved by the Translations Committee of the American Bible Society. The line drawings were especially prepared by Miss Annie Vallotton to accompany the text.

# THE GOSPEL OF LUKE

## Introduction

1 Dear Theophilus:
Many have done their best to write a report of the things that have taken place among us. [2]They wrote what we have been told by those who saw these things from the beginning and proclaimed the message. [3]And so, your Excellency, because I have carefully studied all these matters from their beginning, I thought it good to write an orderly account for you. [4]I do this so that you will know the full truth of all those matters which you have been taught.

## The Birth of John the Baptist Announced

[5]During the time when Herod was king of the land of Israel, there was a priest named Zechariah, who belonged to the priestly order of Abijah. His wife's name was Elizabeth; she also belonged to a priestly family. [6]They both lived good lives in God's sight, and obeyed fully all the Lord's commandments and rules. [7]They had no children because Elizabeth could not have any, and she and Zechariah were both very old.

[8]One day Zechariah was doing his work as a priest before God, taking his turn in the daily service. [9]According to the custom followed by the priests, he was chosen by lot to burn the incense on the altar. So he went into the temple of the Lord, [10]while the crowd of people outside prayed during the hour of burning the incense. [11]An angel of the Lord appeared to him, standing at the right side of the altar where the incense was burned. [12]When Zechariah saw him he was troubled and felt afraid. [13]But the angel said to him, "Don't be afraid, Zechariah! God has heard your

*Don't be afraid, Zechariah!*

1

prayer, and your wife Elizabeth will bear you a son. You are to name him John. [14]How glad and happy you will be, and how happy many others will be when he is born! [15]He will be a great man in the Lord's sight. He must not drink any wine or strong drink. From his very birth he will be filled with the Holy Spirit. [16]He will bring back many of the people of Israel to the Lord their God. [17]He will go ahead of him, strong and mighty like the prophet Elijah. He will bring fathers and children together again; he will turn the disobedient people back to the way of thinking of the righteous; he will get the Lord's people ready for him."

[18]Zechariah said to the angel, "How shall I know if this is so? I am an old man and my wife also is old."

[19]"I am Gabriel," the angel answered. "I stand in the presence of God, who sent me to speak to you and tell you this good news. [20]But you have not believed my message, which will come true at the right time. Because you have not believed you will be unable to speak; you will remain silent until the day my promise to you comes true."

[21]In the meantime the people were waiting for Zechariah, wondering why he was spending such a long time in the temple. [22]When he came out he could not speak to them, and so they knew that he had seen a vision in the temple. Unable to say a word, he made signs to them with his hands.

[23]When his period of service in the temple was over, Zechariah went back home. [24]Some time later his wife Elizabeth became pregnant, and did not leave the house for five months. [25]"Now at last the Lord has helped me in this way," she said. "He has taken away my public disgrace!"

## The Birth of Jesus Announced

[26]In the sixth month of Elizabeth's pregnancy God sent the angel Gabriel to a town in Galilee named Nazareth. [27]He had a message for a girl promised in marriage to a man named Joseph, who was a descendant of King David. The girl's name was Mary. [28]The angel came to her and said, "Peace be with you! The Lord is with you, and has greatly blessed you!"

29Mary was deeply troubled by the angel's message, and she wondered what his words meant. 30The angel said to her, "Don't be afraid, Mary, because God has been gracious to you. 31You will become pregnant and give birth to a son, and you will name him Jesus. 32He will be great and will be called the Son of the Most High God. The Lord God will make him a king, as his ancestor David was, 33and he will be the king of the descendants of Jacob forever; his kingdom will never end!"

34Mary said to the angel, "I am a virgin. How, then, can this be?"

35The angel answered, "The Holy Spirit will come on you, and God's power will rest upon you. For this reason the holy child will be called the Son of God. 36Remember your relative Elizabeth. It is said that she cannot have children; but she herself is now six months pregnant, even though she is very old. 37For there is not a thing that God cannot do."

38"I am the Lord's servant," said Mary; "may it happen to me as you have said." And the angel left her.

## Mary Visits Elizabeth

39Soon afterward Mary got ready and hurried off to the hill country, to a town in Judea. 40She went into Zechariah's house and greeted Elizabeth. 41When Elizabeth heard Mary's greeting, the baby moved within her. Elizabeth was filled with the Holy Spirit, 42and spoke in a loud voice, "You are the most blessed of all women, and blessed is the child you will bear! 43Why should this great thing happen to me, that my Lord's mother comes to visit me? 44For as soon as I heard your greeting, the baby within me jumped with gladness. 45How happy are you to believe that the Lord's message to you will come true!"

## Mary's Song of Praise

46Mary said,
    "My heart praises the Lord;
47    my soul is glad because of God my Savior,
48    because he has remembered me, his lowly
       servant!
    From now on all people will call me happy,

<sup>49</sup> because of the great things the Mighty
      God has done for me.
   His name is holy;
<sup>50</sup> he shows mercy to those who fear him,
      from one generation to another.
<sup>51</sup> He stretched out his mighty arm
      and scattered the proud with all their
      plans.
<sup>52</sup> He brought down mighty kings from their
      thrones,
      and lifted up the lowly.
<sup>53</sup> He filled the hungry with good things,
      and sent the rich away with empty
      hands.
<sup>54</sup> He kept the promise he made to our
      ancestors,
      and came to the help of his servant
      Israel;
<sup>55</sup> he remembered to show mercy to Abra-
      ham
      and to all his descendants forever!"

<sup>56</sup>Mary stayed about three months with Elizabeth,
and then went back home.

## The Birth of John the Baptist

<sup>57</sup>The time came for Elizabeth to have her baby, and
she gave birth to a son. <sup>58</sup>Her neighbors and relatives
heard how wonderfully good the Lord had been to her,
and they all rejoiced with her.

<sup>59</sup>When the baby was a week old they came to circum-
cise him; they were going to name him Zechariah, his
father's name. <sup>60</sup>But his mother said, "No! His name
will be John."

<sup>61</sup>They said to her, "But you don't have any relative
with that name!" <sup>62</sup>Then they made signs to his father,
asking him what name he would like the boy to have.

<sup>63</sup>Zechariah asked for a writing pad and wrote, "His
name is John." How surprised they all were! <sup>64</sup>At that
moment Zechariah was able to speak again, and he
started praising God. <sup>65</sup>The neighbors were all filled
with fear, and the news about these things spread
through all the hill country of Judea. <sup>66</sup>Everyone who

heard of it thought about it and asked, "What is this child going to be?" It was plain that the Lord's power was with him.

## Zechariah's Prophecy

<sup>67</sup>John's father Zechariah was filled with the Holy Spirit, and he spoke God's message,

<sup>68</sup> "Let us praise the Lord, the God of Israel!
He came to the help of his people and
set them free.
<sup>69</sup> He provided a mighty Savior for us,
who is a descendant of his servant
David.
<sup>70</sup> Long ago by means of his holy prophets
he said this:
<sup>71</sup> he promised to save us from our ene-
mies,
and from the power of all those who
hate us.
<sup>72</sup> He said he would show mercy to our
ancestors,
and remember his sacred covenant.
<sup>73-74</sup> He made a solemn promise to our ances-
tor Abraham,
and vowed that he would rescue us
from our enemies,
and allow us to serve him without fear;
<sup>75</sup> to be holy and righteous before him,
all the days of our life.

<sup>76</sup> "You, my child, will be called a prophet of
the Most High God.
You will go ahead of the Lord
to prepare his road for him;
<sup>77</sup> to tell his people that they will be saved,
by having their sins forgiven.
<sup>78</sup> Our God is merciful and tender.
He will cause the bright dawn of salvation to rise on us,
<sup>79</sup> and shine from heaven on all those
who live in the dark shadow of
death,
to guide our steps into the path of
peace."

⁸⁰The child grew and developed in body and spirit. He lived in the desert until the day when he would appear publicly to the people of Israel.

## The Birth of Jesus
*(Also Matt. 1.18–25)*

2 At that time Emperor Augustus sent out an order for all the citizens of the Empire to register themselves for the census. ²When this first census took place, Quirinius was the governor of Syria. ³Everyone, then, went to register himself, each to his own town.

⁴Joseph went from the town of Nazareth, in Galilee, to Judea, to the town named Bethlehem, where King David was born. Joseph went there because he was a descendant of David. ⁵He went to register himself with

*Everyone, then, went to register himself*

Mary, who was promised in marriage to him. She was pregnant, ⁶and while they were in Bethlehem, the time came for her to have her baby. ⁷She gave birth to her first son, wrapped him in cloths and laid him in a manger— there was no room for them to stay in the inn.

## The Shepherds and the Angels

⁸There were some shepherds in that part of the country who were spending the night in the fields, taking care of their flocks. ⁹An angel of the Lord appeared to them, and the glory of the Lord shone over them. They were terribly afraid, ¹⁰but the angel said to them, "Don't be

afraid! I am here with good news for you, which will bring great joy to all the people. ¹¹This very day in David's town your Savior was born—Christ the Lord! ¹²What will prove it to you is this: you will find a baby wrapped in cloths and lying in a manger."

¹³Suddenly a great army of heaven's angels appeared with the angel, singing praises to God,

¹⁴ "Glory to God in the highest heaven,
    and peace on earth to those with
    whom he is pleased!"

¹⁵When the angels went away from them back into heaven, the shepherds said to one another, "Let us go to Bethlehem and see this thing that has happened, that the Lord has told us."

¹⁶So they hurried off and found Mary and Joseph, and saw the baby lying in the manger. ¹⁷When the shepherds saw him they told them what the angel had said about this child. ¹⁸All who heard it were filled with wonder at what the shepherds told them. ¹⁹Mary remembered all these things and thought deeply about them. ²⁰The shepherds went back, singing praises to God for all they had heard and seen; it had been just as the angel had told them.

*Glory to God in the highest heaven*

## Jesus Is Named

²¹A week later, when the time came for the baby to be circumcised, he was named Jesus, the name which the angel had given him before he had been conceived.

## Jesus Is Presented in the Temple

²²The time came for Joseph and Mary to do what the Law of Moses commanded and perform the ceremony of purification. So they took the child to Jerusalem to present him to the Lord,²³as it is written in the law of the Lord, "Every firstborn male shall be dedicated to the Lord." ²⁴They also went to offer a sacrifice of a pair of doves or two young pigeons, as required by the law of the Lord.

²⁵Now there was a man living in Jerusalem whose name was Simeon. He was a good and God-fearing man, and was waiting for Israel to be saved. The Holy Spirit was with him, ²⁶and he had been assured by the Holy Spirit that he would not die before he had seen the Lord's promised Messiah. ²⁷Led by the Spirit, Simeon went into the temple. When the parents brought the child Jesus into the temple to do for him what the Law required, ²⁸Simeon took the child in his arms, and gave thanks to God:

²⁹ "Now, Lord, you have kept your promise,
    and you may let your servant go in
        peace.
³⁰ With my own eyes I have seen your salva-
        tion,
³¹    which you have prepared in the pres-
        ence of all peoples:
³² A light to reveal your way to the Gentiles,
    and bring glory to your people Israel."

³³The child's father and mother were amazed at the things Simeon said about him. ³⁴Simeon blessed them and said to Mary, his mother, "This child is chosen by God for the destruction and the salvation of many in Israel. He will be a sign from God which many people will speak against, ³⁵and so reveal their secret thoughts.

And sorrow, like a sharp sword, will break your own heart."

³⁶There was a prophetess named Anna, daughter of Phanuel, of the tribe of Asher. She was an old woman who had been married for seven years, ³⁷and then had been a widow for eighty-four years. She never left the temple; day and night she worshiped God, fasting and praying. ³⁸That very same hour she arrived and gave thanks to God, and spoke about the child to all who were waiting for God to redeem Jerusalem.

## The Return to Nazareth

³⁹When they had finished doing all that was required by the law of the Lord, they returned to Galilee, to their home town of Nazareth. ⁴⁰The child grew and became strong; he was full of wisdom, and God's blessings were with him.

## The Boy Jesus in the Temple

⁴¹Every year the parents of Jesus went to Jerusalem for the Feast of Passover. ⁴²When Jesus was twelve years old, they went to the feast as usual. ⁴³When the days of the feast were over, they started back home, but the boy Jesus stayed in Jerusalem. His parents did not know this; ⁴⁴they thought that he was with the group, so they traveled a whole day, and then started looking for him among their relatives and friends. ⁴⁵They did not find him, so they went back to Jerusalem looking for him. ⁴⁶On the third day they found him in the temple, sitting with the Jewish teachers, listening to them and asking questions. ⁴⁷All who heard him were amazed at his intelligent answers. ⁴⁸His parents were amazed when they saw him, and his mother said to him, "Son, why have you done this to us? Your father and I have been terribly worried trying to find you."

⁴⁹He answered them, "Why did you have to look for me? Didn't you know that I had to be in my Father's house?" ⁵⁰But they did not understand what he said to them.

⁵¹So Jesus went back with them to Nazareth, where he was obedient to them. His mother treasured all these

*They found him in the temple*

things in her heart. ⁵²And Jesus grew, both in body and in wisdom, gaining favor with God and men.

## The Preaching of John the Baptist
*(Also Matt. 3.1–12; Mark 1.1–8; John 1.19–28)*

3 It was the fifteenth year of the rule of Emperor Tiberius; Pontius Pilate was governor of Judea, Herod was ruler of Galilee, and his brother Philip ruler of the territory of Iturea and Trachonitis; Lysanias was ruler of Abilene, ²and Annas and Caiaphas were high priests. It was at this time that the word of God came to John, the son of Zechariah, in the desert. ³So John went throughout the whole territory of the Jordan River. "Turn away from your sins and be baptized," he preached, "and God will forgive your sins." ⁴As the prophet Isaiah had written in his book,

> "Someone is shouting in the desert:
> 'Get the Lord's road ready for him;
> make a straight path for him to travel!
> ⁵ All low places must be filled up,
> all hills and mountains leveled off.
> The winding roads must be made straight,
> and the rough paths made smooth.
> ⁶ All mankind will see God's salvation!'"

[7]Crowds of people came out to John to be baptized by him. "You snakes!" he said to them. "Who told you that you could escape from God's wrath that is about to come? [8]Do the things that will show that you have turned from your sins. And don't start saying among yourselves, 'Abraham is our ancestor.' I tell you that God can take these rocks and make descendants for Abraham! [9]The ax is ready to cut down the trees at the roots; every tree that does not bear good fruit will be cut down and thrown in the fire."

[10]The people asked him, "What are we to do, then?"

[11]He answered, "Whoever has two shirts must give one to the man who has none, and whoever has food must share it."

[12]Some tax collectors came to be baptized, and they asked him, "Teacher, what are we to do?"

[13]"Don't collect more than is legal," he told them.

[14]Some soldiers also asked him, "What about us? What are we to do?"

He said to them, "Don't take money from anyone by force or accuse anyone falsely. Be content with your pay."

[15]People's hopes began to rise, and they began to wonder about John, thinking that perhaps he might be the Messiah. [16]So John said to all of them, "I baptize you with water, but one who is much greater than I is coming. I am not good enough even to untie his sandals. He will baptize you with the Holy Spirit and fire. [17]He has his winnowing shovel with him, to thresh out all the grain and gather the wheat into his barn; but he will burn the chaff in a fire that never goes out."

[18]In many different ways John urged the people as he preached the Good News to them. [19]But John spoke against Governor Herod, because he had married Herodias, his brother's wife, and had done many other evil things. [20]Then Herod did an even worse thing by putting John in prison.

## The Baptism of Jesus
(Also Matt. 3.13–17; Mark 1.9–11)

[21]After all the people had been baptized, Jesus also was baptized. While he was praying, heaven was opened, [22]and the Holy Spirit came down upon him in

bodily form, like a dove. And a voice came from heaven,
"You are my own dear Son. I am well pleased with you."

## The Genealogy of Jesus
(Also Matt. 1.1–17)

²³When Jesus began his work he was about thirty
years old; he was the son, so people thought, of Joseph,
who was the son of Heli, ²⁴the son of Matthat, the son
of Levi, the son of Melchi, the son of Jannai, the son of
Joseph, ²⁵the son of Mattathias, the son of Amos, the
son of Nahum, the son of Esli, the son of Naggai, ²⁶the
son of Maath, the son of Mattathias, the son of Semein,
the son of Josech, the son of Joda, ²⁷the son of Joanan,
the son of Rhesa, the son of Zerubbabel, the son of
Shealtiel, the son of Neri, ²⁸the son of Melchi, the son
of Addi, the son of Cosam, the son of Elmadam, the son
of Er, ²⁹the son of Joshua, the son of Eliezer, the son of
Jorim, the son of Matthat, the son of Levi, ³⁰the son of
Simeon, the son of Judah, the son of Joseph, the son
of Jonam, the son of Eliakim, ³¹the son of Melea, the son
of Menna, the son of Mattatha, the son of Nathan, the
son of David, ³²the son of Jesse, the son of Obed, the son
of Boaz, the son of Salmon, the son of Nahshon, ³³the
son of Amminadab, the son of Admin, the son of Arni,
the son of Hezron, the son of Perez, the son of Judah,
³⁴the son of Jacob, the son of Isaac, the son of Abraham,
the son of Terah, the son of Nahor, ³⁵the son of Serug,
the son of Reu, the son of Peleg, the son of Eber, the son
of Shelah, ³⁶the son of Cainan, the son of Arphaxad, the
son of Shem, the son of Noah, the son of Lamech, ³⁷the
son of Methuselah, the son of Enoch, the son of Jared,
the son of Mahalaleel, the son of Cainan, ³⁸the son of
Enos, the son of Seth, the son of Adam, the son of God.

## The Temptation of Jesus
(Also Matt. 4.1–11; Mark 1.12–13)

4 Jesus returned from the Jordan full of the Holy
Spirit, and was led by the Spirit into the desert,
²where he was tempted by the Devil for forty days. In
all that time he ate nothing, so that he was hungry when
it was over.

³The Devil said to him, "If you are God's Son, order this stone to turn into bread."

⁴Jesus answered, "The scripture says, 'Man cannot live on bread alone.'"

⁵Then the Devil took him up and showed him in a second all the kingdoms of the world. ⁶"I will give you all this power, and all this wealth," the Devil told him. "It was all handed over to me and I can give it to anyone I choose. ⁷All this will be yours, then, if you kneel down before me."

⁸Jesus answered, "The scripture says, 'Worship the Lord your God and serve only him!'"

⁹Then the Devil took him to Jerusalem and set him on the highest point of the temple, and said to him, "If you are God's Son, throw yourself down from here. ¹⁰For the scripture says, 'God will order his angels to take good care of you.' ¹¹It also says, 'They will hold you up with their hands so that not even your feet will be hurt on the stones.'"

¹²Jesus answered him, "The scripture says, 'You must not put the Lord your God to the test.'"

¹³When the Devil finished tempting Jesus in every way, he left him for a while.

## Jesus Begins His Work in Galilee
*(Also Matt. 4.12–17; Mark 1.14–15)*

¹⁴Then Jesus returned to Galilee, and the power of the Holy Spirit was with him. The news about him spread throughout all that territory. ¹⁵He taught in their synagogues and was praised by all.

## Jesus Rejected at Nazareth
*(Also Matt. 13.53–58; Mark 6.1–6)*

¹⁶Then Jesus went to Nazareth, where he had been brought up, and on the Sabbath day he went as usual to the synagogue. He stood up to read the Scriptures, ¹⁷and was handed the book of the prophet Isaiah. He unrolled the scroll and found the place where it is written,

¹⁸ "The Spirit of the Lord is upon me,
   because he has chosen me to preach the
      Good News to the poor.
   He has sent me to proclaim liberty to
      the captives,

and recovery of sight to the blind;
to set free the oppressed,
<sup>19</sup>    and announce the year when the Lord
will save his people."

<sup>20</sup>Jesus rolled up the scroll, gave it back to the attendant, and sat down. All the people in the synagogue had their eyes fixed on him. <sup>21</sup>He began speaking to them, "This passage of scripture has come true today, as you heard it being read."

<sup>22</sup>They were all well impressed with him, and marveled at the beautiful words that he spoke. They said, "Isn't he the son of Joseph?"

<sup>23</sup>He said to them, "I am sure that you will quote this proverb to me, 'Doctor, heal yourself.' You will also say to me, 'Do here in your own home town the same things we were told happened in Capernaum.' <sup>24</sup>I tell you this," Jesus added. "A prophet is never welcomed in his own home town. <sup>25</sup>Listen to me: it is true that there were many widows in Israel during the time of Elijah, when there was no rain for three and a half years and there was a great famine throughout the whole land. <sup>26</sup>Yet Elijah was not sent to a single one of them, but only to a widow of Zarephath, in the territory of Sidon. <sup>27</sup>And there were many lepers in Israel during the time of the prophet Elisha; yet not one of them was made clean, but only Naaman the Syrian."

<sup>28</sup>All the people in the synagogue were filled with anger when they heard this. <sup>29</sup>They rose up, dragged Jesus out of town, and took him to the top of the hill on which their town was built, to throw him over the cliff. <sup>30</sup>But he walked through the middle of the crowd and went his way.

## A Man with an Evil Spirit
*(Also Mark 1.21–28)*

<sup>31</sup>Then Jesus went to Capernaum, a town in Galilee, where he taught the people on the Sabbath. <sup>32</sup>They were all amazed at the way he taught, because his words had authority. <sup>33</sup>There was a man in the synagogue who had the spirit of an evil demon in him; he screamed out in a loud voice, <sup>34</sup>"Ah! What do you want with us, Jesus of Nazareth? Are you here to destroy us? I know who you are: you are God's holy messenger!"

³⁵Jesus commanded the spirit, "Be quiet, and come out of the man!" The demon threw the man down in front of them and went out of him without doing him any harm.

³⁶They were all amazed, and said to one another, "What kind of words are these? With authority and power this man gives orders to the evil spirits, and they come out!" ³⁷And the report about Jesus spread everywhere in that region.

## Jesus Heals Many People
(Also Matt. 8.14–17; Mark 1.29–34)

³⁸Jesus left the synagogue and went to Simon's home. Simon's mother-in-law was sick with a high fever, and they spoke to Jesus about her. ³⁹He went and stood at her bedside, and gave a command to the fever. The fever left her, and she got up at once and began to wait on them.

⁴⁰After sunset, all who had friends who were sick with various diseases brought them to Jesus; he placed his hands on every one of them and healed them all. ⁴¹Demons, also, went out from many people, screaming, "You are the Son of God!"

Jesus commanded them and would not let them speak, because they knew that he was the Messiah.

## Jesus Preaches in the Synagogues
(Also Mark 1.35–39)

⁴²At daybreak Jesus left the town and went off to a lonely place. The people started looking for him, and when they found him they tried to keep him from leaving. ⁴³But he said to them, "I must preach the Good News of the Kingdom of God in other towns also, because that is what God sent me to do."

⁴⁴So he preached in the synagogues all over the country.

## Jesus Calls the First Disciples
(Also Matt. 4.18–22; Mark 1.16–20)

5 One time Jesus was standing on the shore of Lake Gennesaret while the people pushed their way up to him to listen to the word of God. ²He saw two boats pulled up on the beach; the fishermen had left them and

*Let your nets down for a catch*

were washing the nets. ³Jesus got into one of the boats
—it belonged to Simon—and asked him to push off a
little from the shore. Jesus sat in the boat and taught the
crowd.

⁴When he finished speaking, he said to Simon, "Push
the boat out further to the deep water, and you and
your partners let your nets down for a catch."

⁵"Master," Simon answered, "we worked hard all
night long and caught nothing. But if you say so, I will
let down the nets." ⁶They let the nets down and
caught such a large number of fish that the nets were
about to break. ⁷So they motioned to their partners in
the other boat to come and help them. They came and
filled both boats so full of fish that they were about to
sink. ⁸When Simon Peter saw what had happened, he
fell on his knees before Jesus and said, "Go away from
me, Lord! I am a sinful man!"

⁹He and the others with him were all amazed at the
large number of fish they had caught. ¹⁰The same was
true of Simon's partners, James and John, the sons of
Zebedee. Jesus said to Simon, "Don't be afraid; from
now on you will be catching men."

¹¹They pulled the boats on the beach, left everything,
and followed Jesus.

## Jesus Makes a Leper Clean
*(Also Matt. 8.1–4; Mark 1.40–45)*

¹²Once Jesus was in a certain town where there was a man who was covered with leprosy. When he saw Jesus, he threw himself down and begged him, "Sir, if you want to, you can make me clean!"

¹³Jesus reached out and touched him. "I do want to," he answered. "Be clean!" At once the leprosy left the man. ¹⁴Jesus ordered him, "Don't tell this to anyone, but go straight to the priest and let him examine you; then offer the sacrifice, as Moses ordered, to prove to everyone that you are now clean."

¹⁵But the news about Jesus spread all the more widely, and crowds of people came to hear him and be healed from their diseases. ¹⁶But he would go away to lonely places, where he prayed.

*Let him down on his bed into the middle of the group*

## Jesus Heals a Paralyzed Man
*(Also Matt. 9.1–8; Mark 2.1–12)*

¹⁷One day when Jesus was teaching, some Pharisees and teachers of the Law were sitting there who had come from every town in Galilee and Judea, and from

Jerusalem. The power of the Lord was present for Jesus to heal the sick. [18]Some men came carrying a paralyzed man on a bed, and they tried to take him into the house and lay him before Jesus. [19]Because of the crowd, however, they could find no way to take him in. So they carried him up on the roof, made an opening in the tiles, and let him down on his bed into the middle of the group in front of Jesus. [20]When Jesus saw how much faith they had, he said to the man, "Your sins are forgiven you, my friend."

[21]The teachers of the Law and the Pharisees began to say to themselves, "Who is this man who speaks against God in this way? No man can forgive sins; God alone can!"

[22]Jesus knew their thoughts and said to them, "Why do you think such things? [23]Is it easier to say, 'Your sins are forgiven you,' or to say, 'Get up and walk'? [24]I will prove to you, then, that the Son of Man has authority on earth to forgive sins." So he said to the paralyzed man, "I tell you, get up, pick up your bed, and go home!"

[25]At once the man got up before them all, took the bed he had been lying on, and went home, praising God. [26]They were all completely amazed! Full of fear, they praised God, saying, "What marvelous things we have seen today!"

## Jesus Calls Levi
*(Also Matt. 9.9–13; Mark 2.13–17)*

[27]After this, Jesus went out and saw a tax collector named Levi, sitting in his office. Jesus said to him, "Follow me." [28]Levi got up, left everything, and followed him.

[29]Then Levi had a big feast in his house for Jesus, and there was a large number of tax collectors and other people at the table with them. [30]Some Pharisees and teachers of the Law who belonged to their group complained to Jesus' disciples. "Why do you eat and drink with tax collectors and outcasts?" they asked.

[31]Jesus answered them, "People who are well do not need a doctor, but only those who are sick. [32]I have not come to call the respectable people to repent, but the outcasts."

## The Question about Fasting
*(Also Matt. 9.14–17; Mark 2.18–22)*

³³Some people said to Jesus, "The disciples of John fast frequently and offer up prayers, and the disciples of the Pharisees do the same; but your disciples eat and drink."

³⁴Jesus answered, "Do you think you can make the guests at a wedding party go without food as long as the bridegroom is with them? Of course not! ³⁵But the time will come when the bridegroom will be taken away from them, and they will go without food in those days."

³⁶Jesus told them this parable also, "No one tears a piece off a new coat to patch up an old coat. If he does, he will have torn the new coat, and the piece of new cloth will not match the old. ³⁷Nor does anyone pour new wine into used wineskins. If he does, the new wine will burst the skins, the wine will pour out, and the skins will be ruined. ³⁸No! New wine should be poured into fresh skins! ³⁹And no one wants new wine after drinking old wine. 'The old is better,' he says."

## The Question about the Sabbath
*(Also Matt. 12.1–8; Mark 2.23–28)*

6 Jesus was walking through some wheat fields on a Sabbath day. His disciples began to pick the heads of wheat, rub them in their hands, and eat the grain. ²Some Pharisees said, "Why are you doing what our Law says you cannot do on the Sabbath?"

³Jesus answered them, "Haven't you read what David did when he and his men were hungry? ⁴He went into the house of God, took the bread offered to God, ate it, and gave it also to his men. Yet it is against our Law for anyone to eat it except the priests."

⁵And Jesus concluded, "The Son of Man is Lord of the Sabbath."

## The Man with a Crippled Hand
*(Also Matt. 12.9–14; Mark 3.1–6)*

⁶On another Sabbath Jesus went into a synagogue and taught. A man was there whose right hand was crippled. ⁷Some teachers of the Law and Pharisees wanted some

reason to accuse Jesus of doing wrong; so they watched him very closely to see if he would cure on the Sabbath. [8]But Jesus knew their thoughts and said to the man with the crippled hand, "Stand up and come here to the front." The man got up and stood there. [9]Then Jesus said to them, "I ask you: What does our Law allow us to do on the Sabbath? To help or to harm? To save a man's life or destroy it?" [10]He looked around at them all, then said to the man, "Stretch out your hand." He did so, and his hand became well again.

[11]But they were filled with rage and began to discuss among themselves what they could do to Jesus.

## Jesus Chooses the Twelve Apostles
(Also Matt. 10.1–4; Mark 3.13–19)

[12]At that time Jesus went up a hill to pray, and spent the whole night there praying to God. [13]When day came he called his disciples to him and chose twelve of them, whom he named apostles: [14]Simon (whom he also named Peter) and his brother Andrew; James and John, Philip and Bartholomew, [15]Matthew and Thomas, James, the son of Alphaeus, and Simon (who was called the Patriot), [16]Judas, the son of James, and Judas Iscariot, who became the traitor.

## Jesus Teaches and Heals
(Also Matt. 4.23–25)

[17]Coming down from the hill with them, Jesus stood on a level place with a large number of his disciples. A great crowd of people was there from all over Judea, and from Jerusalem, and from the coast cities of Tyre and Sidon; [18]they came to hear him and to be healed of their diseases. Those who were troubled by evil spirits also came and were healed. [19]All the people tried to touch him, for power was going out from him and healing them all.

## Happiness and Sorrow
(Also Matt. 5.1–12)

[20]Jesus looked at his disciples and said,
   "Happy are you poor;
      the Kingdom of God is yours!
   [21]"Happy are you who are hungry now;

you will be filled!

"Happy are you who weep now;
you will laugh!

[22]"Happy are you when men hate you, and reject you, and insult you, and say that you are evil, because of the Son of Man! [23]Be glad when that happens, and dance for joy, because a great reward is kept for you in heaven. For their ancestors did the very same things to the prophets.

[24] "But how terrible for you who are rich now;
you have had your easy life!

[25] "How terrible for you who are full now;
you will go hungry!

"How terrible for you who laugh now;
you will mourn and weep!

[26]"How terrible when all men speak well of you; because their ancestors said the very same things to the false prophets."

## Love for Enemies
*(Also Matt. 5.38–48; 7.12a)*

[27]"But I tell you who hear me: Love your enemies, do good to those who hate you, [28]bless those who curse you, and pray for those who mistreat you. [29]If anyone hits you on one cheek, let him hit the other one too; if someone takes your coat, let him have your shirt as well. [30]Give to everyone who asks you for something, and when someone takes what is yours, do not ask for it back. [31]Do for others just what you want them to do for you.

[32]"If you love only the people who love you, why should you receive a blessing? Even sinners love those who love them! [33]And if you do good only to those who do good to you, why should you receive a blessing? Even sinners do that! [34]And if you lend only to those from whom you hope to get it back, why should you receive a blessing? Even sinners lend to sinners, to get back the same amount! [35]No! Love your enemies and do good to them; lend and expect nothing back. You will have a great reward, and you will be sons of the Most High God. For he is good to the ungrateful and the wicked. [36]Be merciful, just as your Father is merciful."

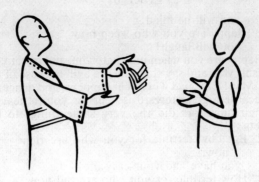

*Lend and expect nothing back*

## Judging Others
*(Also Matt. 7.1–5)*

37"Do not judge others, and God will not judge you; do not condemn others, and God will not condemn you; forgive others, and God will forgive you. 38Give to others, and God will give to you: you will receive a full measure, a generous helping, poured into your hands—all that you can hold. The measure you use for others is the one God will use for you."

39And Jesus told them this parable, "One blind man cannot lead another one; if he does, both will fall into a ditch. 40No pupil is greater than his teacher; but every pupil, when he has completed his training, will be like his teacher.

41"Why do you look at the speck in your brother's eye, but pay no attention to the log in your own eye? 42How can you say to your brother, 'Please, brother, let me take that speck out of your eye,' yet not even see the log in your own eye? You hypocrite! Take the log out of your own eye first, and then you will be able to see and take the speck out of your brother's eye."

## A Tree and Its Fruit
*(Also Matt. 7.16–20; 12.33–35)*

43"A healthy tree does not bear bad fruit, nor does a poor tree bear good fruit. 44Every tree is known by the fruit it bears; you do not pick figs from thorn bushes, or gather grapes from bramble bushes. [45]A good man brings good out of the treasure of good things in his heart; a bad man brings bad out of his treasure of bad things. For a man's mouth speaks what his heart is full of."

## The Two House Builders
(Also Matt. 7.24–27)

[46]"Why do you call me, 'Lord, Lord,' and don't do what I tell you? [47]Everyone who comes to me, and listens to my words, and obeys them—I will show you what he is like. [48]He is like a man who built a house: he dug deep and laid the foundation on the rock. The river flooded over and hit that house but could not shake it, because it had been well built. [49]But the one who hears my words and does not obey them is like a man who built a house on the ground, without laying a foundation; when the flood hit that house it fell at once—what a terrible crash that was!"

## Jesus Heals a Roman Officer's Servant
(Also Matt. 8.5–13)

7 When Jesus had finished saying all these things to the people, he went to Capernaum. [2]A Roman officer there had a servant who was very dear to him; the man was sick and about to die. [3]When the officer heard about Jesus, he sent to him some Jewish elders to ask him to come and heal his servant. [4]They came to Jesus and begged him earnestly, "This man really deserves your help. [5]He loves our people and he himself built a synagogue for us."

[6]So Jesus went with them. He was not far from the house when the officer sent friends to tell him, "Sir, don't trouble yourself. I do not deserve to have you come into my house, [7]neither do I consider myself worthy to come to you in person. Just give the order and my servant will get well. [8]I, too, am a man placed under the authority of superior officers, and I have soldiers under me. I order this one, 'Go!' and he goes; I order that one, 'Come!' and he comes; and I order my slave, 'Do this!' and he does it."

[9]Jesus was surprised when he heard this; he turned around and said to the crowd following him, "I have

never found such faith as this, I tell you, not even in Israel!"

¹⁰The messengers went back to the officer's house and found his servant well.

## Jesus Raises a Widow's Son

¹¹Soon afterward Jesus went to a town named Nain; his disciples and a large crowd went with him. ¹²Just as he arrived at the gate of the town, a funeral procession was coming out. The dead man was the only son of a woman who was a widow, and a large crowd from the city was with her. ¹³When the Lord saw her his heart was filled with pity for her and he said to her, "Don't cry." ¹⁴Then he walked over and touched the coffin, and the men carrying it stopped. Jesus said, "Young man! Get up, I tell you!" ¹⁵The dead man sat up and began to talk, and Jesus gave him back to his mother.

¹⁶Everyone was filled with fear, and they praised God, "A great prophet has appeared among us!" and, "God has come to save his people!"

¹⁷This news about Jesus went out through all the country and the surrounding territory.

## The Messengers from John the Baptist
*(Also Matt. 11.2–19)*

¹⁸John's disciples told him about all these things. He called two of them to him ¹⁹and sent them to the Lord to ask him, "Are you the one John said was going to come, or should we expect someone else?"

²⁰When they came to Jesus they said, "John the Baptist sent us to ask, 'Are you the one he said was going to come, or should we expect someone else?'"

²¹At that very time Jesus healed many people from their sicknesses, diseases, and evil spirits, and gave sight to many blind people. ²²He answered John's messengers, "Go back and tell John what you have seen and heard: the blind can see, the lame can walk, the lepers are made clean, the deaf can hear, the dead are raised to life, and the Good News is preached to the poor. ²³How happy is he who has no doubts about me!"

²⁴After John's messengers had left, Jesus began to speak about John to the crowds, "When you went out to John in the desert, what did you expect to see? A

blade of grass bending in the wind? ²⁵What did you go out to see? A man dressed up in fancy clothes? Really, those who dress like that and live in luxury are found in palaces! ²⁶Tell me, what did you go out to see? A prophet? Yes, I tell you—you saw much more than a prophet. ²⁷For John is the one of whom the scripture says, 'Here is my messenger, says God; I will send him ahead of you to open the way for you.' ²⁸I tell you," Jesus added, "John is greater than any man ever born; but he who is least in the Kingdom of God is greater than he."

²⁹All the people and the tax collectors heard him; they were the ones who had obeyed God's righteous demands and had been baptized by John. ³⁰But the Pharisees and the teachers of the Law rejected God's purpose for themselves, and refused to be baptized by John.

³¹"Now, to what can I compare the people of this day? What are they like? ³²They are like children sitting in the market place. One group shouts to the other, 'We played wedding music for you, but you would not dance! We sang funeral songs, but you would not cry!' ³³John the Baptist came, and he fasted and drank no wine, and you said, 'He has a demon in him!' ³⁴The Son of Man came, and he ate and drank, and you said, 'Look at this man! He is a glutton and wine-drinker, a friend of tax collectors and outcasts!' ³⁵God's wisdom, however, is shown to be true by all who accept it."

## Jesus at the Home of Simon the Pharisee

³⁶A Pharisee invited Jesus to have dinner with him. Jesus went to his house and sat down to eat. ³⁷There was a woman in that town who lived a sinful life. She heard that Jesus was eating in the Pharisee's house, so she brought an alabaster jar full of perfume ³⁸and stood behind Jesus, by his feet, crying and wetting his feet with her tears. Then she dried his feet with her hair, kissed them, and poured the perfume on them. ³⁹When the Pharisee who had invited Jesus saw this, he said to himself, "If this man really were a prophet, he would know who this woman is who is touching him; he would know what kind of sinful life she leads!"

⁴⁰Jesus spoke up and said to him, "Simon, I have something to tell you."

"Yes, Teacher," he said, "tell me."

⁴¹"There were two men who owed money to a money-lender," Jesus began; "one owed him five hundred dollars and the other one fifty dollars. ⁴²Neither one could pay him back, so he canceled the debts of both. Which one, then, will love him more?"

⁴³"I suppose," answered Simon, "that it would be the one who was forgiven more."

"Your answer is correct," said Jesus. ⁴⁴Then he turned to the woman and said to Simon, "Do you see this woman? I came into your home, and you gave me no water for my feet, but she has washed my feet with her tears and dried them with her hair. ⁴⁵You did not wel-

*She has covered my feet with perfume*

come me with a kiss, but she has not stopped kissing my feet since I came. ⁴⁶You provided no oil for my head, but she has covered my feet with perfume. ⁴⁷I tell you, then, the great love she has shown proves that her many sins have been forgiven. Whoever has been forgiven little, however, shows only a little love."

⁴⁸Then Jesus said to the woman, "Your sins are forgiven."

⁴⁹The others sitting at the table began to say to themselves, "Who is this, who even forgives sins?"
⁵⁰But Jesus said to the woman, "Your faith has saved you; go in peace."

## Women Who Accompanied Jesus

8 Some time later Jesus traveled through towns and villages, preaching the Good News about the Kingdom of God. The twelve disciples went with him, ²and so did some women who had been healed of evil spirits and diseases: Mary (who was called Magdalene), from whom seven demons had been driven out; ³Joanna, the wife of Chuza who was an officer in Herod's court; and Susanna, and many other women who used their own resources to help Jesus and his disciples.

## The Parable of the Sower
*(Also Matt. 13.1–9; Mark 4.1–9)*

⁴People kept coming to Jesus from one town after another; and when a great crowd gathered, Jesus told this parable.
⁵"A man went out to sow his seed. As he scattered the seed in the field, some of it fell along the path, where it was stepped on, and the birds ate it up. ⁶Some of it fell on rocky ground, and when the plants sprouted they dried up, because the soil had no moisture. ⁷Some of the seed fell among thorns, which grew up with the plants and choked them. ⁸And some seeds fell in good soil; the plants grew and bore grain, one hundred grains each."
And Jesus concluded, "Listen, then, if you have ears to hear with!"

## The Purpose of the Parables
*(Also Matt. 13.10–17; Mark 4.10–12)*

⁹His disciples asked Jesus what this parable meant.
¹⁰Jesus answered, "The knowledge of the secrets of the Kingdom of God has been given to you; but to the rest it comes by means of parables, so that they may look but not see, and listen but not understand."

## Jesus Explains the Parable of the Sower
*(Also Matt. 13.18–23; Mark 4.13–20)*

¹¹"This is what the parable means: the seed is the

word of God. [12]The seed that fell along the path stands for those who hear; but the Devil comes and takes the message away from their hearts to keep them from believing and being saved. [13]The seed that fell on rocky ground stands for those who hear the message and receive it gladly. But it does not sink deep into them; they believe only for a while, and fall away when the time of testing comes. [14]The seed that fell among thorns stands for those who hear; but the worries and riches and pleasures of this life crowd in and choke them, and their fruit never ripens. [15]The seed that fell in good soil stands for those who hear the message and retain it in a good and obedient heart, and persist until they bear fruit."

## A Lamp under a Bowl
(Also Mark 4.21–25)

[16]"No one lights a lamp and covers it with a bowl or puts it under a bed. Instead, he puts it on the lampstand, so that people will see the light as they come in. [17]Whatever is hidden away will be brought out into the open, and whatever is covered up will be found and brought to light.

[18]"Be careful, then, how you listen; because whoever has something will be given more, but whoever has nothing will have taken away from him even the little he thinks he has."

## Jesus' Mother and Brothers
(Also Matt. 12.46–50; Mark 3.31–35)

[19]Jesus' mother and brothers came to him, but were unable to join him because of the crowd. [20]Someone said to Jesus, "Your mother and brothers are standing outside and want to see you."

[21]Jesus said to them all, "My mother and brothers are those who hear the word of God and obey it."

## Jesus Calms a Storm
(Also Matt. 8.23–27; Mark 4.35–41)

[22]One day Jesus got into a boat with his disciples and said to them, "Let us go across to the other side of the lake." So they started out. [23]As they were sailing, Jesus went to sleep. A strong wind blew down on the lake, and the boat began to fill with water, putting them all in great

danger. ²⁴The disciples came to Jesus and woke him up, saying, "Master, Master! We are about to die!"

Jesus got up and gave a command to the wind and to the stormy water; they quieted down and there was a great calm. ²⁵Then he said to the disciples, "Where is your faith?"

But they were amazed and afraid, and said to one another, "Who is this man? He gives orders to the winds and waves, and they obey him!"

## Jesus Heals a Man with Demons
*(Also Matt. 8.28–34; Mark 5.1–20)*

²⁶They sailed on over to the territory of the Gergesenes, which is across the lake from Galilee. ²⁷As Jesus stepped ashore, he was met by a man from the town who had demons in him. He had gone for a long time without clothes, and would not stay at home, but spent his time in the burial caves. ²⁸When he saw Jesus he gave a loud cry, fell down before him, and said in a loud voice, "Jesus, Son of the Most High God! What do you want with me? I beg you, don't punish me!" ²⁹He said this because Jesus had ordered the evil spirit to go out of him. Many times it had seized him, and even though he was kept a prisoner, his hands and feet tied with chains, he would break the chains and be driven by the demon out into the desert.

³⁰Jesus asked him, "What is your name?"

"My name is 'Mob,' " he answered—because many demons had gone into him. ³¹The demons begged Jesus not to send them into the abyss.

³²A large herd of pigs was near by, feeding on the hillside. The demons begged Jesus to let them go into the pigs, and he let them. ³³So the demons went out of the man and into the pigs; the whole herd rushed down the side of the cliff into the lake and were drowned.

³⁴The men who were taking care of the pigs saw what happened, so they ran off and spread the news in the town and among the farms. ³⁵People went out to see what had happened. They came to Jesus and found the man from whom the demons had gone out sitting at the feet of Jesus, clothed, and in his right mind; and they were all afraid. ³⁶Those who had seen it told the people how the man had been cured. ³⁷Then all the people from

the territory of the Gergesenes asked Jesus to go away, because they were terribly afraid. So Jesus got into the boat and left. 38The man from whom the demons had gone out begged Jesus, "Let me go with you."

But Jesus sent him away, saying, 39"Go back home and tell what God has done for you."

The man went through the whole town telling what Jesus had done for him.

*She told him why she had touched him*

## Jairus' Daughter and the Woman
## Who Touched Jesus' Cloak
(Also Matt. 9.18–26; Mark 5.21–43)

40When Jesus returned to the other side of the lake the crowd welcomed him, because they had all been waiting for him. 41Then a man named Jairus arrived, an official in the local synagogue. He threw himself down at Jesus' feet and begged him to go to his home, 42because his only daughter, twelve years old, was dying.

As Jesus went along, the people were crowding him from every side. 43A certain woman was there who had suffered from severe bleeding for twelve years; she had spent all she had on doctors, but no one had been able to cure her. 44She came up in the crowd behind Jesus and touched the edge of his cloak, and her bleeding stopped at once. ⁴⁵Jesus asked, "Who touched me?"

Everyone denied it, and Peter said, "Master, the people are all around you and crowding in on you."

⁴⁶But Jesus said, "Someone touched me, for I knew it when power went out of me." ⁴⁷The woman saw that she had been found out, so she came, trembling, and threw herself at Jesus' feet. There, in front of everybody, she told him why she had touched him and how she had been healed at once. ⁴⁸Jesus said to her, "My daughter, your faith has made you well. Go in peace."

⁴⁹While Jesus was saying this, a messenger came from the official's house. "Your daughter has died," he told Jairus; "don't bother the Teacher any longer."

⁵⁰But Jesus heard it and said to Jairus, "Don't be afraid; only believe, and she will be well."

⁵¹When he arrived at the house he would not let anyone go in with him except Peter, John, and James, and the child's father and mother. ⁵²Everyone there was crying and mourning for the child. Jesus said, "Don't cry; the child is not dead—she is only sleeping!"

⁵³They all made fun of him, because they knew that she was dead. ⁵⁴But Jesus took her by the hand and called out, "Get up, child!" ⁵⁵Her life returned and she got up at once; and Jesus ordered them to give her something to eat. ⁵⁶Her parents were astounded, but Jesus commanded them not to tell anyone what had happened.

## Jesus Sends Out the Twelve Disciples
*(Also Matt. 10.5–15; Mark 6.7–13)*

9 Jesus called the twelve disciples together and gave them power and authority to drive out all demons and to cure diseases. ²Then he sent them out to preach the Kingdom of God and to heal the sick. ³He said to them, "Take nothing with you for the trip: no walking stick, no beggar's bag, no food, no money, not even an extra shirt. ⁴Wherever you are welcomed, stay in the same house until you leave that town; ⁵wherever people don't welcome you, leave that town and shake the dust off your feet as a warning to them."

⁶The disciples left and traveled through all the vil-

lages, preaching the Good News and healing people everywhere.

## Herod's Confusion
*(Also Matt. 14.1–12; Mark 6.14–29)*

⁷Herod, the ruler of Galilee, heard about all the things that were happening; he was very confused about it because some people were saying, "John the Baptist has come back to life!" ⁸Others said that Elijah had appeared, while others said that one of the prophets of long ago had come back to life. ⁹Herod said, "I had John's head cut off; but who is this man I hear these things about?" And he kept trying to see Jesus.

## Jesus Feeds the Five Thousand
*(Also Matt. 14.13–21; Mark 6.30–44; John 6.1–14)*

¹⁰The apostles came back and told Jesus everything they had done. He took them with him and they went off by themselves to a town named Bethsaida. ¹¹When the crowds heard about it they followed him. He welcomed them, spoke to them about the Kingdom of God, and healed those who needed it.

¹²When the sun had begun to set, the twelve disciples came to him and said, "Send the people away so they can go to the villages and farms around here and find food and lodging, because this is a lonely place."

¹³But Jesus said to them, "You yourselves give them something to eat."

They answered, "All we have is five loaves and two fish. Do you want us to go and buy food for this whole crowd?" ¹⁴(There were about five thousand men there.)

Jesus said to his disciples, "Make the people sit down in groups of about fifty each."

¹⁵The disciples did so and made them all sit down. ¹⁶Jesus took the five loaves and two fish, looked up to heaven, thanked God for them, broke them, and gave them to the disciples to distribute to the people. ¹⁷They all ate and had enough; and the disciples took up twelve baskets of what the people left over.

## Peter's Declaration about Jesus
*(Also Matt. 16.13–19; Mark 8.27–29)*

¹⁸One time when Jesus was praying alone, the disci-

ples came to him. "Who do the crowds say I am?" he asked them.

¹⁹"Some say that you are John the Baptist," they answered. "Others say that you are Elijah, while others say that one of the prophets of long ago has come back to life."

²⁰"What about you?" he asked them. "Who do you say I am?"

Peter answered, "You are God's Messiah."

## Jesus Speaks about His Suffering and Death
(Also Matt. 16.20–28; Mark 8.30—9.1)

²¹Then Jesus gave them strict orders not to tell this to anyone, ²²and added, "The Son of Man must suffer much, and be rejected by the elders, the chief priests, and the teachers of the Law. He will be put to death, and be raised to life on the third day."

²³And he said to all, "If anyone wants to come with me, he must forget himself, take up his cross every day, and follow me. ²⁴For whoever wants to save his own life will lose it; but whoever loses his life for my sake will save it. ²⁵Will a man gain anything if he wins the whole world but is himself lost or defeated? Of course not! ²⁶If a man is ashamed of me and of my teaching, then the Son of Man will be ashamed of him when he comes in his glory and the glory of the Father and of the holy angels. ²⁷Remember this! There are some here, I tell you, who will not die until they have seen the Kingdom of God."

## The Transfiguration
(Also Matt. 17.1–8; Mark 9.2–8)

²⁸About a week after he had said these things, Jesus took Peter, John, and James with him and went up a hill to pray. ²⁹While he was praying, his face changed its appearance and his clothes became dazzling white. ³⁰Suddenly two men were there talking with him. They were Moses and Elijah, ³¹who appeared in heavenly glory and talked with Jesus about how he would soon fulfill God's purpose by dying in Jerusalem.³²Peter and his companions were sound asleep, but they awoke and saw Jesus' glory and the two men who were standing

with him. ³³As the men were leaving Jesus, Peter said to him, "Master, it is a good thing that we are here. We will make three tents, one for you, one for Moses, and one for Elijah." (He really did not know what he was saying.)

³⁴While he was still speaking, a cloud appeared and covered them with its shadow; and the disciples were afraid as the cloud came over them. ³⁵A voice said from the cloud, "This is my Son, whom I have chosen —listen to him!"

³⁶When the voice stopped, there was Jesus all alone. The disciples kept quiet about all this, and told no one at that time anything they had seen.

## Jesus Heals a Boy with an Evil Spirit
(Also Matt. 17.14–18; Mark 9.14–27)

³⁷The next day they went down from the hill, and a large crowd met Jesus. ³⁸A man shouted from the crowd, "Teacher! Look, I beg you, at my son—my only son! ³⁹A spirit attacks him with a sudden shout and throws him into a fit, so that he foams at the mouth; it keeps on hurting him and will hardly let him go! ⁴⁰I begged your disciples to drive it out, but they couldn't."

⁴¹Jesus answered, "How unbelieving and wrong you people are! How long must I stay with you? How long do I have to put up with you?" Then he said to the man, "Bring your son here."

⁴²As the boy was coming, the demon knocked him to the ground and threw him into a fit. Jesus gave a command to the evil spirit, healed the boy, and gave him back to his father. ⁴³All the people were amazed at the mighty power of God.

## Jesus Speaks Again about His Death
(Also Matt. 17.22–23; Mark 9.30–32)

The people were still marveling at everything Jesus was doing, when he said to his disciples, ⁴⁴"Don't forget what I am about to tell you! The Son of Man is going to be handed over to the power of men." ⁴⁵But they did not know what this meant. It had been hidden from them so that they could not understand it, and they were afraid to ask him about the matter.

## Who Is the Greatest?
*(Also Matt. 18.1–5, Mark 9.33–37)*

⁴⁶An argument came up among the disciples as to which one of them was the greatest. ⁴⁷Jesus knew what they were thinking, so he took a child, stood him by his side, ⁴⁸and said to them, "Whoever in my name welcomes this child, welcomes me; and whoever welcomes me, also welcomes the one who sent me. For he who is least among you all is the greatest."

*He who is least among you all is the greatest*

## Who Is not against You Is for You
*(Also Mark 9.38–40)*

⁴⁹John spoke up, "Master, we saw a man driving out demons in your name, and we told him to stop, because he doesn't belong to our group."

⁵⁰"Do not try to stop him," Jesus said to him and to the other disciples, "because whoever is not against you is for you."

## A Samaritan Village Refuses to Receive Jesus

[51] As the days drew near when Jesus would be taken up to heaven, he made up his mind and set out on his way to Jerusalem. [52] He sent messengers ahead of him, who left and went into a Samaritan village to get everything ready for him. [53] But the people there would not receive him, because it was plain that he was going to Jerusalem. [54] When the disciples James and John saw this, they said, "Lord, do you want us to call fire down from heaven and destroy them?"

[55] Jesus turned and rebuked them; [56] and they went on to another village.

## The Would-Be Followers of Jesus

(Also Matt. 8.19–22)

[57] As they went on their way, a certain man said to Jesus, "I will follow you wherever you go."

[58] Jesus said to him, "Foxes have holes, and birds have nests, but the Son of Man has no place to lie down and rest." [59] He said to another man, "Follow me."

But that man said, "Sir, first let me go back and bury my father."

[60] Jesus answered, "Let the dead bury their own dead. You go and preach the Kingdom of God."

[61] Another man said, "I will follow you, sir; but first let me go and say good-bye to my family."

[62] Jesus said to him, "Anyone who starts to plow and then keeps looking back is of no use for the Kingdom of God."

## Jesus Sends Out the Seventy-two

10 After this the Lord chose another seventy-two men and sent them out, two by two, to go ahead of him to every town and place where he himself was about to go. [2] He said to them, "There is a large harvest, but few workers to gather it in. Pray to the owner of the harvest that he will send out workers to gather in his harvest. [3] Go! I am sending you like lambs among wolves. [4] Don't take a purse, or a beggar's bag, or shoes; don't stop to greet anyone on the road. [5] Whenever you go into a house, first say, 'Peace be with this house.' [6] If a peace-loving man lives there, let your greeting of

peace remain on him; if not, take back your greeting of peace. ⁷Stay in that same house, eating and drinking what they offer you, because a worker should be given his pay. Don't move around from one house to another. ⁸Whenever you go into a town and are made welcome, eat what is set before you, ⁹heal the sick in that town, and say to the people there, 'The Kingdom of God has come near you.' ¹⁰But whenever you go into a town and are not welcomed there, go out in the streets and say, ¹¹'Even the dust from your town that sticks to our feet we wipe off against you; but remember this, the Kingdom of God has come near you!' ¹²I tell you that on the Judgment Day God will show more mercy to Sodom than to that town!"

### The Unbelieving Towns
(Also Matt. 11.20–24)

¹³"How terrible it will be for you, Chorazin! How terrible for you too, Bethsaida! If the miracles which were performed in you had been performed in Tyre and Sidon, long ago the people there would have sat down, put on sackcloth, and sprinkled ashes on themselves to show that they had turned from their sins! ¹⁴God will show more mercy on the Judgment Day to Tyre and Sidon than to you. ¹⁵And as for you, Capernaum! You wanted to lift yourself up to heaven? You will be thrown down to hell!"

¹⁶Jesus said to his disciples, "Whoever listens to you, listens to me; whoever rejects you, rejects me; and whoever rejects me, rejects the one who sent me."

### The Return of the Seventy-two

¹⁷The seventy-two men came back in great joy. "Lord," they said, "even the demons obeyed us when we commanded them in your name!"

¹⁸Jesus answered them, "I saw Satan fall like lightning from heaven. ¹⁹Listen! I have given you authority, so that you can walk on snakes and scorpions, and over all the power of the Enemy, and nothing will hurt you. ²⁰But don't be glad because the evil spirits obey you; rather be glad because your names are written in heaven."

## Jesus Rejoices
*(Also Matt. 11.25–27; 13.16–17)*

²¹At that time Jesus was filled with joy by the Holy
Spirit, and said, "Father, Lord of heaven and earth! I
thank you because you have shown to the unlearned
what you have hidden from the wise and learned. Yes,
Father, this was done by your own choice and pleasure.

²²"My Father has given me all things. No one
knows who the Son is except the Father, and no one
knows who the Father is except the Son and those to
whom the Son wants to reveal him."

²³Then Jesus turned to the disciples and said to
them privately, "How fortunate you are, to see the
things you see! ²⁴Many prophets and kings, I tell you,
wanted to see what you see, but they could not, and to
hear what you hear, but they did not."

## The Parable of the Good Samaritan

²⁵A certain teacher of the Law came up and tried to
trap Jesus. "Teacher," he asked, "what must I do to
receive eternal life?"

²⁶Jesus answered him, "What do the Scriptures say?
How do you interpret them?"

²⁷The man answered, " 'You must love the Lord your
God with all your heart, with all your soul, with all your
strength, and with all your mind'; and, 'You must love
your fellow-man as yourself.' "

²⁸"Your answer is correct," replied Jesus; "do this and
you will live."

²⁹But the teacher of the Law wanted to put himself in
the right, so he asked Jesus, "Who is my fellow-man?"

³⁰Jesus answered, "There was a man who was going
down from Jerusalem to Jericho, when robbers attacked
him, stripped him, and beat him up, leaving him half
dead. ³¹It so happened that a priest was going down that
road; when he saw the man he walked on by, on the
other side. ³²In the same way a Levite also came there,
went over and looked at the man, and then walked on
by, on the other side. ³³But a certain Samaritan who was
traveling that way came upon him, and when he saw the

man his heart was filled with pity. ³⁴He went over to him, poured oil and wine on his wounds and bandaged them; then he put the man on his own animal and took him to an inn, where he took care of him. ³⁵The next day he took out two silver coins and gave them to the inn-keeper. 'Take care of him,' he told the innkeeper, 'and when I come back this way I will pay you back whatever you spend on him.' "

³⁶And Jesus concluded, "In your opinion, which one of these three acted like a fellow-man toward the man attacked by the robbers?"

³⁷The teacher of the Law answered, "The one who was kind to him."

Jesus replied, "You go, then, and do the same."

*His heart was filled with pity*

## Jesus Visits Martha and Mary

³⁸As Jesus and his disciples went on their way, he came to a certain village where a woman named Martha welcomed him in her home. ³⁹She had a sister named Mary, who sat down at the feet of the Lord and listened to his teaching. ⁴⁰Martha was upset over all the work she had to do; so she came and said, "Lord, don't you care that my sister has left me to do all the work by myself? Tell her to come and help me!"

⁴¹The Lord answered her, "Martha, Martha! You are worried and troubled over so many things, ⁴²but just one is needed. Mary has chosen the right thing, and it will not be taken away from her."

## Jesus' Teaching on Prayer
(Also Matt. 6.9–13; 7.7–11)

11 One time Jesus was praying in a certain place. When he finished, one of his disciples said to him, "Lord, teach us to pray, just as John taught his disciples."

²Jesus said to them, "This is what you should pray:
'Father:
    May your holy name be honored;
    may your Kingdom come.
³   Give us day by day the food we need.
⁴   Forgive us our sins,
        because we forgive everyone who
        does us wrong.
    And do not bring us to hard testing.' "

⁵And Jesus said to his disciples, "Suppose one of you should go to a friend's house at midnight and tell him, 'Friend, let me borrow three loaves of bread. ⁶A friend of mine who is on a trip has just come to my house and I don't have any food for him!' ⁷And suppose your friend should answer from inside, 'Don't bother me! The door is already locked, and my children and I are in bed. I can't get up to give you anything.' ⁸Well, what then? I tell you, even if he will not get up and give you the bread because he is your friend, yet he will get up and give you everything you need because you are not ashamed to keep on asking. ⁹And so I say to you: Ask, and you will receive; seek, and you will find; knock, and

the door will be opened to you. [10]For everyone who asks will receive, and he who seeks will find, and the door will be opened to him who knocks. [11]Would any of you who are fathers give your son a snake when he asks for fish? [12]Or would you give him a scorpion when he asks for an egg? [13]As bad as you are, you know how to give good things to your children. How much more, then, the Father in heaven will give the Holy Spirit to those who ask him!"

## Jesus and Beelzebul
*(Also Matt. 12.22–30; Mark 3.20–27)*

[14]Jesus was driving out a demon that could not talk; when the demon went out, the man began to talk. The crowds were amazed, [15]but some of the people said, "It is Beelzebul, the chief of the demons, who gives him the power to drive them out."

[16]Others wanted to trap him, so they asked him to perform a miracle to show God's approval. [17]But Jesus knew their thoughts and said to them, "Any country that divides itself into groups that fight each other will not last very long; a family divided against itself falls apart. [18]So if Satan's kingdom has groups fighting each other, how can it last? You say that I drive out demons because Beelzebul gives me the power to do so. [19]If this is how I drive them out, how do your followers drive them out? Your own followers prove that you are wrong! [20]No, it is rather by means of God's power that I drive out demons, which proves that the Kingdom of God has already come to you.

[21]"When a strong man, with all his weapons ready, guards his own house, all his belongings are safe. [22]But when a stronger man attacks him and defeats him, he carries away all the weapons the owner was depending on and divides up what he stole.

[23]"Anyone who is not for me is really against me; anyone who does not help me gather is really scattering."

## The Return of the Evil Spirit
*(Also Matt. 12.43–45)*

[24]"When an evil spirit goes out of a man, it travels over dry country looking for a place to rest. If it can't

find one, it says to itself, 'I will go back to my house which I left.' <sup>25</sup>So it goes back and finds the house clean and all fixed up. <sup>26</sup>Then it goes out and brings seven other spirits even worse than itself, and they come and live there. So that man is in worse shape, when it is all over, than he was at the beginning."

## True Happiness

<sup>27</sup>When Jesus had said this, a woman spoke up from the crowd and said to him, "How happy is the woman who bore you and nursed you!"

<sup>28</sup>But Jesus answered, "Rather, how happy are those who hear the word of God and obey it!"

## The Demand for a Miracle
(Also Matt. 12.38–42)

<sup>29</sup>As the people crowded around Jesus he went on to say, "How evil are the people of this day! They ask for a miracle, but none will be given them except the miracle of Jonah. <sup>30</sup>In the same way that the prophet Jonah was a sign for the people of Nineveh, so the Son of Man will be a sign for the people of this day. <sup>31</sup>On the Judgment Day the Queen from the South will stand up and accuse the people of today, because she traveled halfway around the world to listen to Solomon's wise teaching; and there is something here, I tell you, greater than Solomon. <sup>32</sup>On the Judgment Day the people of Nineveh will stand up and accuse you, because they turned from their sins when they heard Jonah preach; and there is something here, I tell you, greater than Jonah!"

## The Light of the Body
(Also Matt. 5.15; 6.22–23)

<sup>33</sup>"No one lights a lamp and then hides it or puts it under a bowl; instead, he puts it on the lampstand, so that people may see the light as they come in. <sup>34</sup>Your eyes are like a lamp for the body. When your eyes are clear your whole body is full of light; but when your eyes are bad your whole body will be in darkness. <sup>35</sup>Be careful, then, that the light in you is not darkness. <sup>36</sup>If, then, your whole body is full of light, with no part of it in

darkness, it will be bright all over, as when a lamp shines on you with its brightness."

## Jesus Accuses the Pharisees and the Teachers of the Law
(Also Matt. 23.1–36; Mark 12.38–40)

37 When Jesus finished speaking, a Pharisee invited him to eat with him; so he went in and sat down to eat. 38 The Pharisee was surprised when he noticed that Jesus had not washed before eating. 39 So the Lord said to him, "Now, then, you Pharisees clean the cup and plate on the outside, but inside you are full of violence and evil. 40 Fools! Did not God, who made the outside, also make the inside? 41 But give what is in your cups and plates to the poor, and everything will be clean for you.

42 "How terrible for you, Pharisees! You give to God one tenth of the seasoning herbs, such as mint and rue and all the other herbs, but you neglect justice and love for God. These you should practice, without neglecting the others.

43 "How terrible for you, Pharisees! You love the reserved seats in the synagogues, and to be greeted with respect in the market places. 44 How terrible for you! You are like unmarked graves which people walk on without knowing it."

45 One of the teachers of the Law said to him, "Teacher, when you say this you insult us too!"

46 Jesus answered, "How terrible for you, too, teachers of the Law! You put loads on men's backs which are hard to carry, but you yourselves will not stretch out a finger to help them carry those loads. 47 How terrible for you! You make fine tombs for the prophets—the very prophets your ancestors murdered. 48 You yourselves admit, then, that you approve of what your

*You put loads on men's backs*

ancestors did; because they murdered the prophets, and you build their tombs. [49]For this reason the Wisdom of God said, 'I will send them prophets and messengers; they will kill some of them and persecute others.' [50]So the people of this time will be punished for the murder of all the prophets killed since the creation of the world, [51]from the murder of Abel to the murder of Zechariah, who was killed between the altar and the holy place. Yes, I tell you, the people of this time will be punished for them all!

[52]"How terrible for you, teachers of the Law! You have kept the key that opens the door to the house of knowledge; you yourselves will not go in, and you stop those who are trying to go in!"

[53]When Jesus left that place the teachers of the Law and the Pharisees began to criticize him bitterly and ask him questions about many things, [54]trying to lay traps for him and catch him in something wrong he might say.

## A Warning against Hypocrisy
(Also Matt. 10.26–27)

**12** As thousands of people crowded together, so that they were stepping on each other, Jesus said first to his disciples, "Be on guard against the yeast of the Pharisees—I mean their hypocrisy. [2]Whatever is covered up will be uncovered, and every secret will be made known. [3]So then, whatever you have said in the dark will be heard in broad daylight, and whatever you have whispered in men's ears in a closed room will be shouted from the housetops."

## Whom to Fear
(Also Matt. 10.28–31)

[4]"I tell you, my friends, do not be afraid of those who kill the body but cannot afterward do anything worse. [5]I will show you whom to fear: fear God who, after killing, has the authority to throw into hell. Yes, I tell you, be afraid of him!

[6]"Aren't five sparrows sold for two pennies? Yet not a single one of them is forgotten by God. [7]Even the hairs of your head have all been numbered. So do not be afraid; you are worth much more than many sparrows!"

## Confessing and Denying Christ

*(Also Matt. 10.32–33; 12.32; 10.19–20)*

[8]"I tell you: whoever declares publicly that he belongs to me, the Son of Man will do the same for him before the angels of God; [9]but whoever denies publicly that he belongs to me, the Son of Man will also deny him before the angels of God.

[10]"Anyone who says a word against the Son of Man can be forgiven; but the one who says evil things against the Holy Spirit will not be forgiven.

[11]"When they bring you to be tried in the synagogues, or before governors or rulers, do not be worried about how you will defend yourself or what you will say. [12]For the Holy Spirit will teach you at that time what you should say."

## The Parable of the Rich Fool

[13]A man in the crowd said to him, "Teacher, tell my brother to divide with me the property our father left us."

[14]Jesus answered him, "Man, who gave me the right to judge, or to divide the property between you two?" [15]And he went on to say to them all, "Watch out, and guard yourselves from all kinds of greed; because a man's true life is not made up of the things he owns, no matter how rich he may be."

[16]Then Jesus told them this parable, "A rich man had land which bore good crops. [17]He began to think to himself, 'I don't have a place to keep all my crops. What can I do? [18]This is what I will do,' he told himself; 'I will tear my barns down and build bigger ones, where I will store the grain and all my other goods. [19]Then I will say to myself, Lucky man! You have all the good things you need for many years. Take life easy, eat, drink, and enjoy yourself!' [20]But God said to him, 'You fool! This very night you will have to give up your life; then who will get all these things you have kept for yourself?' "

[21]And Jesus concluded, "This is how it is with those who pile up riches for themselves but are not rich in God's sight."

## Trust in God
*(Also Matt. 6.25–34)*

22Then Jesus said to the disciples, "This is why I tell you: do not be worried about the food you need to stay alive, or about the clothes you need for your body. 23Life is much more important than food, and body much more important than clothes. 24Look at the crows: they don't plant seeds or gather a harvest; they don't have

*Do not be worried*

storage rooms or barns; God feeds them! You are worth so much more than birds! 25Which one of you can live a few more years by worrying about it? 26If you can't manage even such a small thing, why worry about the other things? 27Look how the wild flowers grow: they don't work or make clothes for themselves. But I tell you that not even Solomon, as rich as he was, had clothes as beautiful as one of these flowers. 28It is God who clothes the wild grass—grass that is here today, gone tomorrow, burned up in the oven. Won't he be all the more sure to clothe you? How little faith you have! 29So don't be all upset, always concerned about what you will eat and drink. 30(For the heathen of this world are always concerned about all these things.) Your Father knows that you need these things. 31Instead, be concerned with his Kingdom, and he will provide you with these things."

## Riches in Heaven
*(Also Matt. 6.19–21)*

32"Do not be afraid, little flock; because your Father is pleased to give you the Kingdom. 33Sell all your belongings and give the money to the poor. Provide for yourselves purses that don't wear out, and save your riches in heaven, where they will never decrease, because no thief can get to them, no moth can destroy them. 34For your heart will always be where your riches are."

## Watchful Servants

35"Be ready for whatever comes, with your clothes fastened tight at the waist and your lamps lit, 36like servants who are waiting for their master to come back from a wedding feast. When he comes and knocks, they will open the door for him at once. 37How happy are those servants whose master finds them awake and ready when he returns! I tell you, he will fasten his belt, have them sit down, and wait on them. 38How happy are they if he finds them ready, even if he should come as late as midnight or even later! 39And remember this! If the man of the house knew the time when the thief would come, he would not let the thief break into his house. 40And you, too, be ready, because the Son of Man will come at an hour when you are not expecting him."

## The Faithful or the Unfaithful Servant
*(Also Matt. 24.45–51)*

41Peter said, "Lord, are you telling this parable to us, or do you mean it for everyone?"

42The Lord answered, "Who, then, is the faithful and wise servant? He is the one whom his master will put in charge, to run the household and give the other servants their share of the food at the proper time. 43How happy is that servant if his master finds him doing this when he comes home! 44Indeed, I tell you, the master will put that servant in charge of all his property. 45But if that servant says to himself, 'My master is taking a long time to come back,' and begins to beat the other servants, both the men and the women, and eats and drinks and

gets drunk, <sup>46</sup>then the master will come back some day
when the servant does not expect him and at a time he
does not know. The master will cut him to pieces, and
make him share the fate of the disobedient.

<sup>47</sup>"The servant who knows what his master wants
him to do, but does not get himself ready and do what
his master wants, will be punished with a heavy whipping; <sup>48</sup>but the servant who does not know what his
master wants, and does something for which he deserves a whipping, will be punished with a light whipping. The man to whom much is given, of him much
is required; the man to whom more is given, of him
much more is required."

## Jesus the Cause of Division
(Also Matt. 10.34–36)

<sup>49</sup>"I came to set the earth on fire; how I wish it were
already kindled! <sup>50</sup>I have a baptism to receive; how dis-
tressed I am until it is over! <sup>51</sup>Do you suppose that I
came to bring peace to the world? Not peace, I tell you,
but division. <sup>52</sup>From now on a family of five will be
divided, three against two, two against three. <sup>53</sup>Fathers
will be against their sons, and sons against their fathers;
mothers will be against their daughters, and daughters
against their mothers; mothers-in-law will be against
their daughters-in-law, and daughters-in-law against
their mothers-in-law."

## Understanding the Time
(Also Matt. 16.2–3)

<sup>54</sup>Jesus said also to the people, "When you see a cloud
coming up in the west, at once you say, 'It is going to
rain,' and it does. <sup>55</sup>And when you feel the south wind
blowing, you say, 'It is going to get hot,' and it does.
<sup>56</sup>Hypocrites! You can look at the earth and the sky and
tell what it means; why, then, don't you know the meaning of this present time?"

## Settle with Your Opponent
(Also Matt. 5.25–26)

<sup>57</sup>"Why do you not judge for yourselves the right
thing to do? <sup>58</sup>If a man brings a lawsuit against you and
takes you to court, do your best to settle the matter with

him while you are on the way, so that he won't drag you before the judge, and the judge hand you over to the police, and the police put you in jail. ⁵⁹You will not come out of there, I tell you, until you pay the last penny of your fine."

## Turn from Your Sins or Die

**13** At that time some people were there who told Jesus about the Galileans whom Pilate had killed while they were offering sacrifices to God. ²Jesus answered them, "Because these Galileans were killed in that way, do you think it proves that they were worse sinners than all the other Galileans? ³No! I tell you that if you do not turn from your sins, you will all die as they did. ⁴What about those eighteen in Siloam who were killed when the tower fell on them? Do you suppose this proves that they were worse than all the other people living in Jerusalem? ⁵No! I tell you that if you do not turn from your sins, you will all die as they did."

## The Parable of the Unfruitful Fig Tree

⁶Then Jesus told them this parable, "A man had a fig tree growing in his vineyard. He went looking for figs on it but found none. ⁷So he said to his gardener, 'Look, for three years I have been coming here looking for figs on this fig tree and I haven't found any. Cut it down! Why should it go on using up the soil?' ⁸But the gardener answered, 'Leave it alone, sir, just this one year; I will dig a trench around it and fill it up with fertilizer. ⁹Then if the tree bears figs next year, so much the better; if not, then you will have it cut down.' "

## Jesus Heals a Crippled Woman on the Sabbath

¹⁰One Sabbath day Jesus was teaching in a synagogue. ¹¹A woman was there who had an evil spirit in her that had kept her sick for eighteen years; she was bent over and could not straighten up at all. ¹²When Jesus saw her he called out to her, "Woman, you are free from your sickness!" ¹³He placed his hands on her and at once she straightened herself up and praised God.

¹⁴The official of the synagogue was angry that Jesus had healed on the Sabbath; so he spoke up and said to the people, "There are six days in which we should

work; so come during those days and be healed, but not on the Sabbath!"

<sup>15</sup>The Lord answered him by saying, "You hypocrites! Any one of you would untie his ox or his donkey from the stall and take it out to give it water on the Sabbath. <sup>16</sup>Now here is this descendant of Abraham whom Satan has kept in bonds for eighteen years; should she not be freed from her bonds on the Sabbath?" <sup>17</sup>His answer made all his enemies ashamed of themselves, while all the people rejoiced over every wonderful thing that he did.

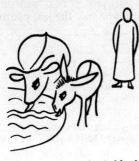

*Give it water on the Sabbath*

## The Parable of the Mustard Seed
*(Also Matt. 13.31–32; Mark 4.30–32)*

<sup>18</sup>Jesus asked, "What is the Kingdom of God like? What shall I compare it with? <sup>19</sup>It is like a mustard seed, which a man took and planted in his field; the plant grew and became a tree, and the birds made their nests in its branches."

## The Parable of the Yeast
*(Also Matt. 13.33)*

<sup>20</sup>Again Jesus asked, "What shall I compare the Kingdom of God with? <sup>21</sup>It is like the yeast which a woman takes and mixes in a bushel of flour, until the whole batch of dough rises."

## The Narrow Door
*(Also Matt. 7.13–14, 21–23)*

<sup>22</sup>Jesus went through towns and villages, teaching and making his way toward Jerusalem. <sup>23</sup>Someone asked him, "Sir, will just a few people be saved?"

Jesus answered them, <sup>24</sup>"Do your best to go in through the narrow door; because many people, I tell you, will try to go in but will not be able. <sup>25</sup>The master of the house will get up and close the door; then when you stand outside and begin to knock on the door and say, 'Open the door for us, sir!' he will answer you, 'I don't know where you come from!' [26]Then you will answer back, 'We ate and drank with you; you taught in our town!' [27]He will say again, 'I don't know where you come from. Get away from me, all you evildoers!' [28]What crying and gnashing of teeth there will be when you see Abraham, Isaac, and Jacob and all the prophets in the Kingdom of God, while you are thrown out! [29]People will come from the east and the west, from the north and the south, and sit at the table in the Kingdom of God. [30]Then those who are now last will be first, and those who are now first will be last."

## Jesus' Love for Jerusalem

*(Also Matt. 23.37–39)*

[31]At that same time some Pharisees came to Jesus and said to him, "You must get out of here and go somewhere else, because Herod wants to kill you."

[32]Jesus answered them, "Go tell that fox: 'I am driving out demons and performing cures today and tomorrow, and on the third day I shall finish my work.' [33]Yet I must be on my way today, tomorrow, and the next day; it is not right for a prophet to be killed anywhere except in Jerusalem.

[34]"Jerusalem, Jerusalem! You kill the prophets, you stone the messengers God has sent you! How many times I wanted to put my arms around all your people, just as a hen gathers her chicks under her wings, but you would not let me! [35]Now your home will be completely forsaken. You will not see me, I tell you, until the time comes when you say, 'God bless him who comes in the name of the Lord.'"

## Jesus Heals a Sick Man

14 One Sabbath day Jesus went to eat a meal at the home of one of the leading Pharisees; and people were watching Jesus closely. [2]A man whose legs and arms were swollen came to Jesus, [3]and Jesus spoke up and asked the teachers of the Law and the Pharisees, "Does our Law allow healing on the Sabbath, or not?"

[4]But they would not say a thing. Jesus took the man, healed him, and sent him away. [5]Then he said to them, "If any one of you had a son or an ox that happened to

fall in a well on a Sabbath, would you not pull him out
at once on the Sabbath itself?"

⁶But they were not able to answer him about this.

## Humility and Hospitality

⁷Jesus noticed how some of the guests were choosing
the best places, so he told this parable to all of them,
⁸"When someone invites you to a wedding feast, do not
sit down in the best place. It could happen that someone
more important than you had been invited, ⁹and your
host, who invited both of you, would come and say to
you, 'Let him have this place.' Then you would be
ashamed and have to sit in the lowest place. ¹⁰Instead,
when you are invited, go and sit in the lowest place, so
that your host will come to you and say, 'Come on up,
my friend, to a better place.' This will bring you honor
in the presence of all the other guests. ¹¹Because everyone who makes himself great will be humbled, and everyone who humbles himself will be made great."

¹²Then Jesus said to his host, "When you give a lunch
or a dinner, do not invite your friends, or your brothers,
or your relatives, or your rich neighbors—because they
will invite you back and in this way you will be paid for
what you did. ¹³When you give a feast, invite the poor,
the crippled, the lame, and the blind, ¹⁴and you will be
blessed; because they are not able to pay you back. You
will be paid by God when the good people rise from
death."

## The Parable of the Great Feast
(Also Matt. 22.1–10)

¹⁵One of the men sitting at the table heard this and
said to Jesus, "How happy are those who will sit at the
table in the Kingdom of God!"

¹⁶Jesus said to him, "There was a man who was giving
a great feast, to which he invited many people. ¹⁷At the
time for the feast he sent his servant to tell his guests,
'Come, everything is ready!' ¹⁸But they all began, one
after another, to make excuses. The first one told the
servant, 'I bought a field, and have to go and look at it;
please accept my apologies.' ¹⁹Another one said, 'I
bought five pairs of oxen and am on my way to try them

out; please accept my apologies.' [20]Another one said, 'I have just gotten married, and for this reason I cannot come.' [21]The servant went back and told all this to his master. The master of the house was furious and said to his servant, 'Hurry out to the streets and alleys of the town, and bring back the poor, the crippled, the blind, and the lame.' [22]Soon the servant said, 'Your order has been carried out, sir, but there is room for more.' [23]So the master said to the servant, 'Go out to the country roads and lanes, and make people come in, so that my house will be full. [24]I tell you all that none of those men who were invited will taste my dinner!' "

## The Cost of Being a Disciple
*(Also Matt. 10.37–38)*

[25]Great crowds of people were going along with Jesus. He turned and said to them, [26]"Whoever comes to me cannot be my disciple unless he hates his father and his mother, his wife and his children, his brothers and his sisters, and himself as well. [27]Whoever does not carry his own cross and come after me cannot be my disciple. [28]If one of you is planning to build a tower, he sits down first and figures out what it will cost, to see if he has enough money to finish the job. [29]If he doesn't, he will not be able to finish the tower after laying the foundation; and all who see what happened will make fun of him. [30]'This man began to build but can't finish the job!' they will say. [31]If a king goes out with ten thousand men to fight another king, who comes against him with twenty thousand men, he will sit down first and decide if he is strong enough to face that other king. [32]If he isn't, he will send messengers to meet the other king, while he is still a long way off, to ask for terms of peace. [33]In the same way," concluded Jesus, "none of you can be my disciple unless he gives up everything he has."

## Worthless Salt
*(Also Matt. 5.13; Mark 9.50)*

[34]"Salt is good, but if it loses its taste there is no way to make it salty again. [35]It is no good for the soil or for the manure pile; it is thrown away. Listen, then, if you have ears!"

## The Lost Sheep
*(Also Matt. 18.12–14)*

**15** One time many tax collectors and outcasts came to listen to Jesus. [2]The Pharisees and the teachers of the Law started grumbling, "This man welcomes outcasts and even eats with them!" [3]So Jesus told them this parable,

[4]"Suppose one of you has a hundred sheep and loses one of them—what does he do? He leaves the other ninety-nine sheep in the pasture and goes looking for the one that got lost until he finds it. [5]When he finds it, he is so happy that he puts it on his shoulders, [6]and carries it back home. Then he calls his friends and neighbors together, and says to them, 'I am so happy I found my lost sheep. Let us celebrate!' [7]In the same way, I tell you, there will be more joy in heaven over one sinner who repents than over ninety-nine respectable people who do not need to repent."

## The Lost Coin

[8]"Or suppose a woman who has ten silver coins loses one of them—what does she do? She lights a lamp, sweeps her house, and looks carefully everywhere until she finds it. [9]When she finds it, she calls her friends and neighbors together, and says to them, 'I am so happy I found the coin I lost. Let us celebrate!' [10]In the same way, I tell you, the angels of God rejoice over one sinner who repents."

## The Lost Son

[11]Jesus went on to say, "There was a man who had two sons. [12]The younger one said to him, 'Father, give me now my share of the property.' So the man divided the property between his two sons. [13]After a few days the younger son sold his part of the property and left home with the

*Left home with the money*

money. He went to a country far away, where he wasted his money in reckless living. ¹⁴He spent everything he had. Then a severe famine spread over that country, and he was left without a thing. ¹⁵So he went to work for one of the citizens of that country, who sent him out to his farm to take care of the pigs. ¹⁶He wished he could fill himself with the bean pods the pigs ate, but no one gave him anything to eat.        ¹⁷At last he came to his senses

*Here I am, about to starve!*

and said, 'All my father's hired workers have more than they can eat, and here I am, about to starve! ¹⁸I will get up and go to my father and say, "Father, I have sinned against God and against you. ¹⁹I am no longer fit to be called your son; treat me as one of your hired workers." '
²⁰So he got up and started back to his father.

"He was still a long way from home when his father saw him; his heart was filled with pity and he ran, threw his arms around his son, and kissed him. ²¹'Father,' the son said, 'I have sinned against God and against you. I am no longer fit to be called your son.' ²²But the father called his servants: 'Hurry!' he said. 'Bring the best robe and put it on him. Put a ring on his finger and shoes on his feet. ²³Then go get the prize calf and kill it, and let us celebrate with a feast! ²⁴Because this son of mine was dead, but now he is alive; he was lost, but now he has been found.' And so the feasting began.

<sup>25</sup>"The older son, in the meantime, was out in the field. On his way back, when he came close to the house, he heard the music and dancing. <sup>26</sup>He called one of the servants and asked him, 'What's going on?' <sup>27</sup>'Your brother came back home,' the servant answered, 'and your father killed the prize calf, because he got him back safe and sound.' <sup>28</sup>The older brother was so angry that he would not go into the house; so his father came out and begged

*He has been found*

him to come in. <sup>29</sup>'Look,' he answered back to his father, 'all these years I have worked like a slave for you, and I never disobeyed your orders. What have you given me? Not even a goat for me to have a feast with my friends! <sup>30</sup>But this son of yours wasted all your property on prostitutes, and when he comes back home you kill the prize calf for him!' <sup>31</sup>'My son,' the father answered, 'you are always here with me and everything I have is yours. <sup>32</sup>But we had to have a feast and be happy, because your brother was dead, but now he is alive; he was lost, but now he has been found.' "

## The Shrewd Manager

**16** Jesus said to his disciples, "There was a rich man who had a manager, and he was told that the manager was wasting his master's money. <sup>2</sup>He called him in and said, 'What is this I hear about you? Turn in a complete account of your handling of my property, because you cannot be my manager any longer.' <sup>3</sup>'My master is going to dismiss me from my job,' the man said to himself. 'What shall I do? I am not strong enough to dig ditches, and I am ashamed to beg. <sup>4</sup>Now I know what I will do! Then when my job is gone I shall have friends who will welcome me in their homes.' ⁵So he called in all the people who were in debt to his master. He said to the first one, 'How much do you owe my master?' ⁶'One hundred barrels of olive oil,' he answered. 'Here is your account,' the manager told him; 'sit down and write fifty.' ⁷He said to another one, 'And you—how much do you owe?' 'A thousand bushels of wheat,' he answered. 'Here is your account,' the manager told him; 'write eight hundred.' ⁸The master of this dishonest manager praised him for doing such a shrewd thing; because the people of this world are much more shrewd in handling their affairs than the people who belong to the light.'

⁹And Jesus went on to say, "And so I tell you: make friends for yourselves with worldly wealth, so that when it gives out you will be welcomed in the eternal home. ¹⁰Whoever is faithful in small matters will be faithful in large ones; whoever is dishonest in small matters will be dishonest in large ones. ¹¹If, then, you have not been faithful in handling worldly wealth, how can you be trusted with true wealth? ¹²And if you have not been faithful with what belongs to someone else, who will give you what belongs to you?

¹³"No servant can be the slave of two masters; he will hate one and love the other; he will be loyal to one and despise the other. You cannot serve both God and money."

## Some Sayings of Jesus
(Also Matt. 11.12-13; 5.31-32; Mark 10.11-12)

¹⁴The Pharisees heard all this, and they made fun of Jesus, because they loved money. ¹⁵Jesus said to them, "You are the ones who make yourselves look right in men's sight, but God knows your hearts. For what men think is of great value is worth nothing in God's sight.

¹⁶"The Law of Moses and the writings of the prophets were in effect up to the time of John the Baptist; since then the Good News about the Kingdom of God is being told, and everyone forces his way in. ¹⁷But it is easier for heaven and earth to disappear than for the smallest detail of the Law to be done away with.

¹⁸"Any man who divorces his wife and marries an-

other woman commits adultery; and the man who marries a divorced woman commits adultery."

## The Rich Man and Lazarus

[19]"There was once a rich man who dressed in the most expensive clothes and lived in great luxury every day. [20]There was also a poor man, named Lazarus, full of sores, who used to be brought to the rich man's door, [21]hoping to fill himself with the bits of food that fell from the rich man's table. Even the dogs would come and lick his sores. [22]The poor man died and was carried by the angels to Abraham's side, at the feast in heaven; the rich man died and was buried. [23]He was in great pain in Hades; and he looked up and saw Abraham, far away, with Lazarus at his side. [24]So he called out, 'Father Abraham! Take pity on me, and send Lazarus to dip his finger in some water and cool off my tongue, because I am in great pain in this fire!' [25]But Abraham said, 'Remember, my son, that in your lifetime you were given all the good things, while Lazarus got all the bad things; but now he is enjoying himself here, while you are in pain. [26]Besides all that, there is a deep pit lying between us, so that those who want to cross over from here to you cannot do it, nor can anyone cross over to us from where you are.' [27]The rich man said, 'Well, father, I beg you, send Lazarus to my father's house, [28]where I have five brothers; let him go and warn them so that they, at least, will not come to this place of pain.' [29]Abraham said, 'Your brothers have Moses and the prophets to warn them; let your brothers listen to what they say.' [30]The rich man answered, 'That is not enough, father Abraham! But if someone were to rise from death and go to them, then they would turn from their sins.' [31]But Abraham said, 'If they will not listen to Moses and the prophets, they will not be convinced even if someone were to rise from death.'"

## Sin
*(Also Matt. 18.6–7, 21–22; Mark 9.42)*

**17** Jesus said to his disciples, "Things that make people fall into sin are bound to happen; but how terrible for the one who makes them happen! [2]It would be better for him if a large millstone were tied around his neck and he were thrown into the sea, than for him to cause one of these little ones to sin. ³Be on your guard!

"If your brother sins, rebuke him, and if he repents, forgive him. ⁴If he sins against you seven times in one day, and each time he comes to you saying, 'I repent,' you must forgive him."

## Faith

⁵The apostles said to the Lord, "Make our faith greater."

⁶The Lord answered, "If you had faith as big as a mustard seed, you could say to this mulberry tree, 'Pull yourself up by the roots and plant yourself in the sea!' and it would obey you."

## A Servant's Duty

⁷"Suppose one of you has a servant who is plowing or looking after the sheep. When he comes in from the field, do you say to him, 'Hurry along and eat your meal'? ⁸Of course not! Instead, you say to him, 'Get my supper ready, then put on your apron and wait on me while I eat and drink; after that you may eat and drink.' ⁹The servant does not deserve thanks for obeying orders, does he? ¹⁰It is the same with you; when you have done all you have been told to do, say, 'We are ordinary servants; we have only done our duty.' "

## Jesus Makes Ten Lepers Clean

¹¹As Jesus made his way to Jerusalem he went between Samaria and Galilee. ¹²He was going into a village when he was met by ten lepers. They stood at a distance ¹³and shouted, "Jesus! Master! Have pity on us!"

¹⁴Jesus saw them and said to them, "Go and let the priests examine you."

On the way they were made clean. ¹⁵One of them, when he saw that he was healed, came back, praising God in a loud voice. ¹⁶He threw himself to the ground at Jesus' feet, thanking him. The man was a Samaritan. ¹⁷Jesus spoke up, "There were ten men made clean;

where are the other nine? [18]Why is this foreigner the only one who came back to give thanks to God?" [19]And Jesus said to him, "Get up and go; your faith has made you well."

*Where are the other nine?*

## The Coming of the Kingdom
(Also Matt. 24.23–28, 37–41)

[20]Some Pharisees asked Jesus when the Kingdom of God would come. His answer was, "The Kingdom of God does not come in such a way as to be seen. [21]No one will say, 'Look, here it is!' or, 'There it is!'; because the Kingdom of God is within you."

[22]Then he said to the disciples, "The time will come when you will wish you could see one of the days of the Son of Man, but you will not see it. [23]There will be those who will say to you, 'Look, over there!' or, 'Look, over here!' But don't go out looking for it. [24]As the lightning flashes across the sky and lights it up from one side to

the other, so will the Son of Man be in his day. 25But first he must suffer much and be rejected by the people of this day. 26As it was in the time of Noah, so shall it be in the days of the Son of Man. 27Everybody kept on eating and drinking, men and women married, up to the very day Noah went into the ark and the Flood came and killed them all. 28It will be as it was in the time of Lot. Everybody kept on eating and drinking, buying and selling, planting and building. 29On the day Lot left Sodom, fire and sulfur rained down from heaven and killed them all. 30That is how it will be on the day the Son of Man is revealed.

31"The man who is on the roof of his house on that day must not go down into the house to get his belongings that are there; in the same way, the man who is out in the field must not go back to the house. 32Remember Lot's wife! 33Whoever tries to save his own life will lose it; whoever loses his life will save it. 34On that night, I tell you, there will be two men sleeping in one bed: one will be taken away, the other left behind. 35Two women will be grinding meal together: one will be taken away, the other left behind. [36Two men will be in the field: one will be taken away, the other left behind.]"

37The disciples asked him, "Where, Lord?"

Jesus answered, "Where there is a dead body the vultures will gather."

### The Parable of the Widow and the Judge

**18** Then Jesus told them this parable, to teach them that they should always pray and never become discouraged. 2"There was a judge in a certain town who neither feared God nor respected men. 3And there was a widow in that same town who kept coming to him and pleading for her rights: 'Help me against my opponent!' 4For a long time the judge was not willing, but at last he said to himself, 'Even though I don't fear God or respect men, 5yet because of all the trouble this widow is giving me I will see to it that she gets her rights; or else she will keep on coming and finally wear me out!' "

6And the Lord continued, "Listen to what that corrupt judge said. 7Now, will God not judge in favor of his own people who cry to him for help day and night? Will he be slow to help them? [8]I tell you, he will judge in their favor, and do it quickly. But will the Son of Man find faith on earth when he comes?"

## The Parable of the Pharisee and the Tax Collector

[9]Jesus also told this parable to people who were sure of their own goodness and despised everybody else. [10]"Two men went up to the temple to pray; one was a Pharisee, the other a tax collector. [11]The Pharisee stood apart by himself and prayed, 'I thank you, God, that I am not greedy, dishonest, or immoral, like everybody else; I thank you that I am not like that tax collector. [12]I fast two days every week, and I give you one tenth of all my income.' [13]But the tax collector stood at a distance and would not even raise his face to heaven, but beat on his breast and said, 'God, have pity on me, a sinner!' [14]I tell you," said Jesus, "this man, and not the other, was in the right with God when he went home. Because everyone who makes himself great will be humbled, and everyone who humbles himself will be made great."

## Jesus Blesses Little Children
*(Also Matt. 19.13–15; Mark 10.13–16)*

[15]Some people brought their babies to Jesus to have him place his hands on them. But the disciples saw them and scolded them for doing so. [16]But Jesus called the children to him, and said, "Let the children come to me, and do not stop them, because the Kingdom of God belongs to such as these. [17]Remember this! Whoever does not receive the Kingdom of God like a child will never enter it."

## The Rich Man
*(Also Matt. 19.16–30; Mark 10.17–31)*

[18]A Jewish leader asked Jesus, "Good Teacher, what must I do to receive eternal life?"

[19]"Why do you call me good?" Jesus asked him. "No one is good except God alone. [20]You know the commandments: 'Do not commit adultery; do not murder; do not steal; do not lie; honor your father and mother.' "

²¹The man replied, "Ever since I was young I have obeyed all these commandments."

²²When Jesus heard this, he said to him, "You still need to do one thing. Sell all you have and give the money to the poor, and you will have riches in heaven; then come and follow me." ²³But when the man heard this he became very sad, because he was very rich.

²⁴Jesus saw that he was sad and said, "How hard it is for rich people to enter the Kingdom of God! ²⁵It is much harder for a rich man to enter the Kingdom of God than for a camel to go through the eye of a needle."

²⁶The people who heard him asked, "Who, then, can be saved?"

²⁷Jesus answered, "What is impossible for men is possible for God."

²⁸Then Peter said, "Look! We have left our homes to follow you."

²⁹"Yes," Jesus said to them, "and I tell you this: anyone who leaves home or wife or brothers or parents or children for the sake of the Kingdom of God ³⁰will receive much more in this present age, and eternal life in the age to come."

## Jesus Speaks a Third Time about His Death
(Also Matt. 20.17–19; Mark 10.32–34)

³¹Jesus took the twelve disciples aside and said to them, "Listen! We are going to Jerusalem where everything the prophets wrote about the Son of Man will come true. ³²He will be handed over to the Gentiles, who will make fun of him, insult him, and spit on him. ³³They will whip him and kill him, but on the third day he will rise to life."

³⁴The disciples did not understand any of these things; the meaning of the words was hidden from them, and they did not know what Jesus was talking about.

## Jesus Heals a Blind Beggar
(Also Matt. 20.29–34; Mark 10.46–52)

³⁵Jesus was coming near Jericho, and a certain blind man was sitting by the road, begging. ³⁶When he heard the crowd passing by he asked, "What is this?"

³⁷"Jesus of Nazareth is passing by," they told him.

³⁸He cried out, "Jesus! Son of David! Have mercy on me!"

³⁹The people in front scolded him and told him to be quiet. But he shouted even more loudly, "Son of David! Have mercy on me!"

⁴⁰So Jesus stopped and ordered that the blind man be brought to him. When he came near, Jesus asked him, ⁴¹"What do you want me to do for you?"

"Sir," he answered, "I want to see again."

⁴²Then Jesus said to him, "See! Your faith has made you well."

⁴³At once he was able to see, and he followed Jesus, giving thanks to God. When the crowd saw it, they all praised God.

### Jesus and Zacchaeus

19 Jesus went on into Jericho and was passing through. ²There was a chief tax collector there, named Zacchaeus, who was rich. ³He was trying to see

*He was a little man*

who Jesus was, but he was a little man and could not see Jesus because of the crowd. ⁴So he ran ahead of the crowd and climbed a sycamore tree to see Jesus, who would be going that way. ⁵When Jesus came to that place, he looked up and said to Zacchaeus, "Hurry down, Zacchaeus, because I must stay in your house today."

⁶Zacchaeus hurried down and welcomed him with great joy. ⁷All the people who saw it started grumbling, "This man has gone as a guest to the home of a sinner!"

⁸Zacchaeus stood up and said to the Lord, "Listen, sir! I will give half my belongings to the poor; and if I have cheated anyone, I will pay him back four times as much."

⁹Jesus said to him, "Salvation has come to this house today; this man, also, is a descendant of Abraham. ¹⁰For the Son of Man came to seek and to save the lost."

## The Parable of the Gold Coins
(Also Matt. 25.14–30)

¹¹While the people were listening to this, Jesus continued and told them a parable. He was now almost at Jerusalem, and they supposed that the Kingdom of God was just about to appear. ¹²So he said, "There was a nobleman who went to a country far away to be made king and then come back home. ¹³Before he left, he called his ten servants and gave them each a gold coin and told them, 'See what you can earn with this while I am gone.' ¹⁴Now, his countrymen hated him, and so they sent messengers after him to say, 'We don't want this man to be our king.'

¹⁵"The nobleman was made king and came back. At once he ordered his servants, to whom he had given the money, to appear before him in order to find out how much they had earned. ¹⁶The first one came and said, 'Sir, I have earned ten gold coins with the one you gave me.' ¹⁷'Well done,' he said; 'you are a good servant! Since you were faithful in small matters, I will put you in charge of ten cities.' ¹⁸The second servant came and said, 'Sir, I have earned five gold coins with the one you gave me.' ¹⁹To this one he said, 'You will be in charge of five cities.' ²⁰Another servant came and said, 'Sir, here is your gold coin; I kept it hidden in a handkerchief. ²¹I was afraid of you, because you are a

hard man. You take what is not yours, and reap what you did not plant.' <sup>22</sup>He said to him, 'You bad servant! I will use your own words to condemn you! You know that I am a hard man, taking what is not mine and reaping what I have not planted. <sup>23</sup>Well, then, why didn't you put my money in the bank? Then I would have received it back with interest when I returned.' <sup>24</sup>Then he said to those who were standing there, 'Take the gold coin away from him and give it to the servant who has ten coins.' <sup>25</sup>They said to him, 'Sir, he already has ten coins!' <sup>26</sup>'I tell you,' he replied, 'that to every one who has, even more will be given; but the one who does not have, even the little that he has will be taken away from him. <sup>27</sup>Now, as for these enemies of mine who did not want me to be their king: bring them here and kill them before me!' "

*The Master needs it*

## The Triumphant Entry into Jerusalem
*(Also Matt. 21.1–11; Mark 11.1–11; John 12.12–19)*

<sup>28</sup>Jesus said this and then went on to Jerusalem ahead of them. <sup>29</sup>As he came near Bethphage and Bethany, at the Mount of Olives, he sent two disciples ahead <sup>30</sup>with

these instructions, "Go to the village there ahead of you; as you go in you will find a colt tied up that has never been ridden. Untie it and bring it here. ³¹If someone asks you, 'Why are you untying it?' tell him, 'The Master needs it.'"

³²They went on their way and found everything just as Jesus had told them. ³³As they were untying the colt, its owners said to them, "Why are you untying it?"

³⁴"The Master needs it," they answered, ³⁵and took the colt to Jesus. Then they threw their cloaks over the animal and helped Jesus get on. ³⁶As he rode on, they spread their cloaks on the road.

³⁷When he came near Jerusalem, at the place where the road went down the Mount of Olives, the large crowd of his disciples began to thank God and praise him in loud voices for all the great things that they had seen: ³⁸"God bless the king who comes in the name of the Lord! Peace in heaven, and glory to God!"

³⁹Then some of the Pharisees spoke up from the crowd to Jesus. "Teacher," they said, "command your disciples to be quiet!"

⁴⁰Jesus answered, "If they keep quiet, I tell you, the stones themselves will shout."

## Jesus Weeps over Jerusalem

⁴¹He came closer to the city and when he saw it he wept over it, ⁴²saying, "If you only knew today what is needed for peace! But now you cannot see it! ⁴³The days will come upon you when your enemies will surround you with barricades, blockade you, and close in on you from every side. ⁴⁴They will completely destroy you and the people within your walls; not a single stone will they leave in its place, because you did not recognize the time when God came to save you!"

## Jesus Goes to the Temple
(Also Matt. 21.12–17; Mark 11.15–19; John 2.13–22)

⁴⁵Jesus went into the temple and began to drive out the merchants, ⁴⁶saying to them, "It is written in the Scriptures that God said, 'My house will be called a house of prayer.' But you have turned it into a hideout for thieves!"

*God bless the king who comes in the name of the Lord!*

⁴⁷Jesus taught in the temple every day. The chief priests, the teachers of the Law, and the leaders of the people wanted to kill him, ⁴⁸but they could not find how to do it, because all the people kept listening to him, not wanting to miss a single word.

### The Question about Jesus' Authority
(Also Matt. 21.23–27; Mark 11.27–33)

**20** One day, when Jesus was in the temple teaching the people and preaching the Good News, the chief priests and the teachers of the Law, together with the elders, came ²and said to him, "Tell us, what right do you have to do these things? Who gave you the right to do them?"

³Jesus answered them, "Now let me ask you a question. Tell me, ⁴did John's right to baptize come from God or from men?"

⁵They started to argue among themselves, "What shall we say? If we say, 'From God,' he will say, 'Why, then, did you not believe John?' ⁶But if we say, 'From men,' this whole crowd here will stone us, because they are convinced that John was a prophet." ⁷So they answered, "We don't know where it came from."

⁸And Jesus said to them, "Neither will I tell you, then, by what right I do these things."

### The Parable of the Tenants in the Vineyard
(Also Matt. 21.33–46; Mark 12.1–12)

⁹Then Jesus told the people this parable, "A man planted a vineyard, rented it out to tenants, and then left home for a long time. ¹⁰When the time came for harvesting the grapes, he sent a slave to the tenants to receive from them his share of the harvest. But the tenants beat the slave and sent him back without a thing. ¹¹So he sent another slave; but the tenants beat him also, treated him shamefully, and sent him back without a thing. ¹²Then he sent a third slave; the tenants hurt him, too, and threw him out. ¹³Then the owner of the vineyard said, 'What shall I do? I will send my own dear son; surely they will respect him!' ¹⁴But when the tenants saw him they said to one another, 'This is the owner's son. Let us kill him, and his property will be ours!' ¹⁵So they threw him out of the vineyard and killed him.

"What, then, will the owner of the vineyard do to the tenants?" Jesus asked. ¹⁶"He will come and kill those men, and turn over the vineyard to other tenants."

When the people heard this they said, "Surely not!"

¹⁷Jesus looked at them and asked, "What, then, does this scripture mean?

'The very stone which the builders re-
      jected
    turned out to be the most important
      stone.'

[18]Everyone who falls on that stone will be cut to
pieces; and if the stone falls on someone, it will crush
him to dust."

## The Question about Paying Taxes
(Also Matt. 22.15–22; Mark 12.13–17)

[19]The teachers of the Law and the chief priests tried
to arrest Jesus on the spot, because they knew that he
had told this parable against them; but they were afraid
of the people. [20]So they watched for the right time. They
bribed some men to pretend they were sincere, and sent
them to trap Jesus with questions, so they could hand
him over to the authority and power of the Governor.
[21]These spies said to Jesus, "Teacher, we know that
what you say and teach is right. We know that you pay
no attention to a man's status, but teach the truth about
God's will for man. [22]Tell us, is it against our Law for
us to pay taxes to the Roman Emperor, or not?"

[23]But Jesus saw through their trick and said to them,
[24]"Show me a silver coin. Whose face and name are
these on it?"

"The Emperor's," they answered.

[25]So Jesus said, "Well, then, pay to the Emperor what
belongs to him, and pay to God what belongs to God."

[26]They could not catch him in a thing there before the
people, so they kept quiet, amazed at his answer.

## The Question about Rising from Death
(Also Matt. 22.23–33; Mark 12.18–27)

[27]Some Sadducees came to Jesus. (They are the ones
who say that people will not rise from death.) They
asked him, [28]"Teacher, Moses wrote this law for us: 'If
a man dies and leaves a wife, but no children, that man's
brother must marry the widow so they can have children
for the dead man.' [29]Once there were seven brothers; the
oldest got married, and died without having children.
[30]Then the second one married the woman, [31]and then
the third. The same thing happened to all seven—they

died without having children. ³²Last of all, the woman died. ³³Now, on the day when the dead rise to life, whose wife will she be? All seven of them had married her."

³⁴Jesus answered them, "The men and women of this age marry, ³⁵but the men and women who are worthy to rise from death and live in the age to come do not marry. ³⁶They are like angels and cannot die. They are the sons of God, because they have risen from death. ³⁷And Moses clearly proves that the dead are raised to life. In the passage about the burning bush he speaks of the Lord as 'the God of Abraham, the God of Isaac, and the God of Jacob.' ³⁸This means that he is the God of the living, not of the dead, because all are alive to him."

³⁹Some of the teachers of the Law spoke up, "A good answer, Teacher!" ⁴⁰For they did not dare ask him any more questions.

## The Question about the Messiah
(Also Matt. 22.41–46; Mark 12.35–37)

⁴¹Jesus said to them, "How can it be said that the Messiah will be the descendant of David? ⁴²Because David himself says in the book of Psalms,

'The Lord said to my Lord:
    Sit here at my right side,
⁴³    until I put your enemies as a footstool
        under your feet.'

⁴⁴David, then, called him 'Lord.' How can the Messiah be David's descendant?"

## Jesus Warns against the Teachers of the Law
(Also Matt. 23.1–36; Mark 12.38–40)

⁴⁵As all the people listened to him, Jesus said to his disciples, ⁴⁶"Watch out for the teachers of the Law, who like to walk around in their long robes, and love to be greeted with respect in the market place; who choose the reserved seats in the synagogues and the best places at feasts; ⁴⁷who take advantage of widows and rob them of their homes, and then make a show of saying long prayers! Their punishment will be all the worse!"

## The Widow's Offering
*(Also Mark 12.41–44)*

**21** Jesus looked around and saw rich men dropping their gifts in the temple treasury, ²and he also saw a very poor widow dropping in two little copper coins. ³He said, "I tell you that this poor widow put in more than all the others. ⁴For the others offered their gifts from what they had to spare of their riches; but she, poor as she is, gave all she had to live on."

*She, poor as she is, gave all she had to live on*

## Jesus Speaks of the Destruction of the Temple
*(Also Matt. 24.1–2; Mark 13.1–2)*

⁵Some of them were talking about the temple, how beautiful it looked with its fine stones and the gifts offered to God. Jesus said, ⁶"All this you see—the time will come when not a single stone here will be left in its place; every one will be thrown down."

## Troubles and Persecutions
*(Also Matt. 24.3–14; Mark 13.3–13)*

⁷"Teacher," they asked, "when will this be? And what will happen to show that the time has come for it to take place?"

⁸Jesus said, "Watch out; don't be fooled. Because many men will come in my name saying, 'I am he!' and, 'The time has come!' But don't follow them. ⁹Don't be

afraid when you hear of wars and revolutions; such things must happen first, but they do not mean that the end is near."

¹⁰He went on to say, "Countries will fight each other, kingdoms will attack one another. ¹¹There will be terrible earthquakes, famines, and plagues everywhere; there will be awful things and great signs from the sky. ¹²Before all these things take place, however, you will be arrested and persecuted; you will be handed over to trial in synagogues and be put in prison; you will be brought before kings and rulers for my sake. ¹³This will be your chance to tell the Good News. ¹⁴Make up your minds ahead of time not to worry about how you will defend yourselves; ¹⁵because I will give you such words and wisdom that none of your enemies will be able to resist or deny what you say. ¹⁶You will be handed over by your parents, your brothers, your relatives, and your friends; they will put some of you to death. ¹⁷Everyone will hate you because of me. ¹⁸But not a single hair from your heads will be lost. ¹⁹Stand firm, because this is how you will save yourselves."

## Jesus Speaks of the Destruction of Jerusalem
*(Also Matt. 24.15–21; Mark 13.14–19)*

²⁰"When you see Jerusalem surrounded by armies, then you will know that soon she will be destroyed. ²¹Then those who are in Judea must run away to the hills; those who are in the city must leave, and those who are out in the country must not go into the city. ²²For these are 'The Days of Punishment,' to make come true all that the Scriptures say. ²³How terrible it will be in those days for women who are pregnant, and for mothers with little babies! Terrible distress will come upon this land, and God's wrath will be against this people. ²⁴Some will be killed by the sword, and others taken as prisoners to all countries; and the heathen will trample over Jerusalem until their time is up."

## The Coming of the Son of Man
*(Also Matt. 24.29–31; Mark 13.24–27)*

²⁵"There will be signs in the sun, the moon, and the stars. On earth, whole countries will be in despair, afraid

of the roar of the sea and the raging tides. ²⁶Men will faint from fear as they wait for what is coming over the whole earth; for the powers in space will be driven from their courses. ²⁷Then the Son of Man will appear, coming in a cloud with great power and glory. ²⁸When these things begin to happen, stand up and raise your heads, because your salvation is near."

## The Lesson of the Fig Tree
*(Also Matt. 24.32–35; Mark 13.28–31)*

²⁹Then Jesus told them this parable, "Remember the fig tree and all the other trees. ³⁰When you see their leaves beginning to appear you know that summer is near. ³¹In the same way, when you see these things happening, you will know that the Kingdom of God is about to come.

³²"Remember this! All these things will take place before the people now living have all died. ³³Heaven and earth will pass away; my words will never pass away."

## The Need to Watch

³⁴"Watch yourselves! Don't let yourselves become occupied with too much feasting and strong drink, and the worries of this life, or that Day may come on you suddenly. ³⁵For it will come like a trap upon all men over the whole earth. ³⁶Be on watch and pray always that you will have the strength to go safely through all these things that will happen, and to stand before the Son of Man."

³⁷Jesus spent those days teaching in the temple, and when evening came he would go out and spend the night on the Mount of Olives. ³⁸All the people would go to the temple early in the morning to listen to him.

## The Plot against Jesus
*(Also Matt. 26.1–5; Mark 14.1–2; John 11.45–53)*

22 The time was near for the Feast of Unleavened Bread, which is called the Passover. ²The chief priests and the teachers of the Law were trying to find some way of killing Jesus; because they were afraid of the people.

## Judas Agrees to Betray Jesus
*(Also Matt. 26.14–16; Mark 14.10–11)*

³Then Satan went into Judas, called Iscariot, who was one of the twelve disciples. ⁴So Judas went off and spoke with the chief priests and the officers of the temple guard about how he could hand Jesus over to them. ⁵They were pleased and offered to pay him money. ⁶Judas agreed to it and started looking for a good chance to betray Jesus to them without the people knowing about it.

## Jesus Prepares to Eat the Passover Meal
*(Also Matt. 26.17–25; Mark 14.12–21; John 13.21–30)*

⁷The day came during the Feast of Unleavened Bread when the lambs for the Passover meal had to be killed. ⁸Jesus sent Peter and John with these instructions, "Go and get our Passover meal ready for us to eat."

⁹"Where do you want us to get it ready?" they asked him.

¹⁰He said, "Listen! As you go into the city a man carrying a jar of water will meet you. Follow him into the house that he enters, ¹¹and say to the owner of the house: 'The Teacher says to you, Where is the room where my disciples and I will eat the Passover meal?' ¹²He will show you a large furnished room upstairs, where you will get everything ready."

¹³They went off and found everything just as Jesus had told them, and prepared the Passover meal.

## The Lord's Supper
*(Also Matt. 26.26–30; Mark 14.22–26; 1 Cor. 11.23–25)*

¹⁴When the hour came, Jesus took his place at the table with the apostles. ¹⁵He said to them, "I have wanted so much to eat this Passover meal with you before I suffer! ¹⁶For I tell you, I will never eat it until it is given its full meaning in the Kingdom of God."

¹⁷Then Jesus took the cup, gave thanks to God, and said, "Take this and share it among yourselves; ¹⁸for I tell you that I will not drink this wine from now on until the Kingdom of God comes."

¹⁹Then he took the bread, gave thanks to God, broke it, and gave it to them, saying, "This is my body [which

is given for you. Do this in memory of me." ²⁰In the same way he gave them the cup, after the supper, saying, "This cup is God's new covenant sealed with my blood which is poured out for you.]

²¹"But, look! The one who betrays me is here at the table with me! ²²Because the Son of Man will die as God has decided it; but how terrible for that man who betrays him!"

²³Then they began to ask among themselves which one of them it could be who was going to do this.

## The Argument about Greatness

²⁴An argument came up among the disciples as to which one of them should be thought of as the greatest. ²⁵Jesus said to them, "The kings of this world have power over their people, and the rulers are called 'Friends of the People.' ²⁶But this is not the way it is with you; rather, the greatest one among you must be like the youngest, and the leader must be like the servant. ²⁷Who is greater, the one who sits down to eat or the one who serves him? The one who sits down, of course. But I am among you as one who serves.

²⁸"You have stayed with me all through my trials; ²⁹and just as my Father has given me the right to rule, so I will make the same agreement with you. ³⁰You will eat and drink at my table in my Kingdom, and you will sit on thrones to judge the twelve tribes of Israel."

## Jesus Predicts Peter's Denial
(Also Matt. 26.31–35; Mark 14.27–31; John 13.36–38)

³¹"Simon, Simon! Listen! Satan has received permission to test all of you, as a farmer separates the wheat from the chaff. ³²But I have prayed for you, Simon, that your faith will not fail. And when you turn back to me, you must strengthen your brothers."

³³Peter answered, "Lord, I am ready to go to prison with you and to die with you!"

³⁴"I tell you, Peter," Jesus answered, "the rooster will not crow today until you have said three times that you do not know me."

*Simon, Simon! Listen!*

## Purse, Bag, and Sword

<sup>35</sup>Then Jesus said to them, "When I sent you out that time without purse, bag, or shoes, did you lack anything?"

"Not a thing," they answered.

<sup>36</sup>"But now," Jesus said, "whoever has a purse or a bag must take it; and whoever does not have a sword must sell his coat and buy one. <sup>37</sup>For I tell you this: the scripture that says, 'He was included with criminals,' must come true about me. Because that which was written about me is coming true."

<sup>38</sup>The disciples said, "Look! Here are two swords, Lord!"

"That is enough!" he answered.

## Jesus Prays on the Mount of Olives
*(Also Matt. 26.36–46; Mark 14.32–42)*

<sup>39</sup>Jesus left the city and went, as he usually did, to the Mount of Olives; and the disciples went with him. <sup>40</sup>When he came to the place he said to them, "Pray that you will not fall into temptation."

<sup>41</sup>Then he went off from them, about the distance of a stone's throw, and knelt down and prayed. <sup>42</sup>"Father," he said, "if you will, take this cup away from me. Not my will, however, but your will be done." [<sup>43</sup>An angel from heaven appeared to him and strengthened him. <sup>44</sup>In great anguish he prayed even more fervently; his

sweat was like drops of blood, falling to the ground.]

[45]Rising from his prayer, he went back to the disciples and found them asleep, worn out by their grief. [46]And he said to them, "Why are you sleeping? Get up, and pray that you will not fall into temptation."

## The Arrest of Jesus
(Also Matt. 26.47–56; Mark 14.43–50; John 18.3–11)

[47]Jesus was still speaking when a crowd arrived. Judas, one of the twelve disciples, was leading them, and he came up to Jesus to kiss him. [48]But Jesus said, "Is it with a kiss, Judas, that you betray the Son of Man?"

[49]When the disciples who were with Jesus saw what was going to happen, they said, "Shall we strike with our swords, Lord?" [50]And one of them struck the High Priest's slave and cut off his right ear.

[51]But Jesus said, "Enough of this!" He touched the man's ear and healed him.

[52]Then Jesus said to the chief priests and the officers of the temple guard and the elders who had come there to get him, "Did you have to come with swords and clubs, as though I were an outlaw? [53]I was with you in the temple every day, and you did not try to arrest me. But this is your hour to act, when the power of darkness rules."

## Peter Denies Jesus
(Also Matt. 26.57–58, 69–75; Mark 14.53–54, 66–72; John 18.12–18, 25–27)

[54]They arrested Jesus and took him away into the house of the High Priest; and Peter followed from a distance. [55]A fire had been lit in the center of the courtyard, and Peter joined those who were sitting around it. [56]When one of the servant girls saw him sitting there at the fire, she looked straight at him and said, "This man too was with him!"

[57]But Peter denied it, "Woman, I don't even know him!"

[58]After a little while, a man noticed him and said, "You are one of them, too!"

But Peter answered, "Man, I am not!"

[59]And about an hour later another man insisted

*This man too was with him!*

strongly, "There isn't any doubt that this man was with
him, because he also is a Galilean!"

⁶⁰But Peter answered, "Man, I don't know what
you are talking about!"

At once, while he was still speaking, a rooster
crowed. ⁶¹The Lord turned around and looked
straight at Peter, and Peter remembered the Lord's
words, how he had said, "Before the rooster crows
today, you will say three times that you do not
know me." ⁶²Peter went out and wept bitterly.

## Jesus Mocked and Beaten
*(Also Matt. 26.67–68; Mark 14.65)*

⁶³The men who were guarding Jesus made fun of him
and beat him. ⁶⁴They blindfolded him and asked him,
"Who hit you? Guess!" ⁶⁵And they said many other
insulting things to him.

## Jesus before the Council
*(Also Matt. 26.59–66; Mark 14.55–64; John 18.19–24)*

⁶⁶When day came, the elders of the Jews, the chief
priests, and the teachers of the Law met together, and
Jesus was brought to their Council. ⁶⁷"Tell us," they
said, "are you the Messiah?"

He answered, "If I tell you, you will not believe me,
⁶⁸and if I ask you a question you will not answer. ⁶⁹But
from now on the Son of Man will be seated at the right
side of the Almighty God."

⁷⁰They all said, "Are you, then, the Son of God?"
He answered them, "You say that I am."
⁷¹And they said, "We don't need any witnesses! We
ourselves have heard his very own words!"

## Jesus before Pilate
(Also Matt. 27.1–2, 11–14; Mark 15.1–5; John 18.28–38)

23 The whole group rose up and took Jesus before
Pilate, ²where they began to accuse him, "We
caught this man misleading our people, telling them not
to pay taxes to the Emperor and claiming that he himself
is Christ, a king."

³Pilate asked him, "Are you the king of the Jews?"
"You say it," answered Jesus.

⁴Then Pilate said to the chief priests and the crowds,
"I find no reason to condemn this man."

⁵But they insisted even more strongly, "He is starting
a riot among the people all through Judea with his teaching. He began in Galilee, and now has come here."

## Jesus before Herod

⁶When Pilate heard this he asked, "Is this man a
Galilean?" ⁷When he learned that Jesus was from the
region ruled by Herod, he sent him to Herod, who was
also in Jerusalem at that time. ⁸Herod was very pleased
when he saw Jesus, because he had heard about him and
had been wanting to see him for a long time. He was
hoping to see Jesus perform some miracle. ⁹So Herod
asked Jesus many questions, but Jesus did not answer a
word. ¹⁰The chief priests and the teachers of the Law
stepped forward and made strong accusations against
Jesus. ¹¹Herod and his soldiers made fun of Jesus and
treated him with contempt. They put a fine robe on him
and sent him back to Pilate. ¹²On that very day Herod
and Pilate became friends; they had been enemies before
this.

## Jesus Sentenced to Death
(Also Matt. 27.15–26; Mark 15.6–15; John 18.39—19.16)

¹³Pilate called together the chief priests, the leaders,
and the people, ¹⁴and said to them, "You brought this
man to me and said that he was misleading the people.

Now, I have examined him here in your presence, and I have not found him guilty of any of the crimes you accuse him of. ¹⁵Nor did Herod find him guilty, because he sent him back to us. There is nothing this man has done to deserve death. ¹⁶I will have him whipped, then, and let him go."

[¹⁷At each Passover Feast Pilate had to set free one prisoner for them.] ¹⁸The whole crowd cried out, "Kill him! Set Barabbas free for us!" ¹⁹(Barabbas had been put in prison for a riot that had taken place in the city, and for murder.)

²⁰Pilate wanted to set Jesus free, so he called out to the crowd again. ²¹But they shouted back, "To the cross with him! To the cross!"

²²Pilate said to them the third time, "But what crime has he committed? I cannot find anything he has done to deserve death! I will have him whipped and set him free."

²³But they kept on shouting at the top of their voices that Jesus should be nailed to the cross; and finally their shouting won. ²⁴So Pilate passed the sentence on Jesus that they were asking for. ²⁵He set free the man they wanted, the one who had been put in prison for riot and murder, and turned Jesus over to them to do as they wished.

## Jesus Nailed to the Cross
(Also Matt. 27.32–44; Mark 15.21–32; John 19.17–27)

²⁶They took Jesus away. As they went, they met a man named Simon, from Cyrene, who was coming into the city from the country. They seized him, put the cross on him, and made him carry it behind Jesus.

²⁷A large crowd of people followed him; among them were some women who were weeping and·wailing for him. ²⁸Jesus turned to them and said, "Women of Jerusalem! Don't cry for me, but for yourselves and your children. ²⁹For the days are coming when people will say, 'How lucky are the women who never had children, who never bore babies, who never nursed them!' ³⁰That will be the time when people will say to the mountains, 'Fall on us!' and to the hills, 'Hide us!' ³¹For if such things as these are done when the wood is green, what will it be like when it is dry?"

*Put the cross on him and made him carry it*

³²They took two others also, both of them criminals, to be put to death with Jesus. ³³When they came to the place called "The Skull," they nailed Jesus to the cross there, and the two criminals, one on his right and one on his left. ³⁴Jesus said, "Forgive them, Father! They don't know what they are doing."

They divided his clothes among themselves by throwing dice. ³⁵The people stood there watching, while the Jewish leaders made fun of him, "He saved others; let him save himself, if he is the Messiah whom God has chosen!"

³⁶The soldiers also made fun of him; they came up to him and offered him cheap wine, ³⁷and said, "Save yourself, if you are the king of the Jews!"

³⁸These words were written above him: "This is the King of the Jews."

³⁹One of the criminals hanging there hurled insults at him, "Aren't you the Messiah? Save yourself and us!"

⁴⁰The other one, however, rebuked him, saying, "Don't you fear God? We are all under the same sentence. ⁴¹Ours, however, is only right, because we are getting what we deserve for what we did; but he has done no wrong." ⁴²And he said to Jesus, "Remember me, Jesus, when you come as King!"

⁴³Jesus said to him, "I tell you this: today you will be in Paradise with me."

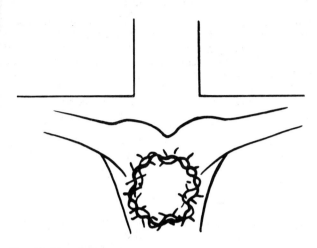

*He said this and died*

## The Death of Jesus
(Also Matt. 27.45–56; Mark 15.33–41; John 19.28–30)

⁴⁴It was about twelve o'clock when the sun stopped shining and darkness covered the whole country until three o'clock; ⁴⁵and the curtain hanging in the temple was torn in two. ⁴⁶Jesus cried out in a loud voice, "Father! In your hands I place my spirit!" He said this and died.

⁴⁷The army officer saw what had happened, and he praised God, saying, "Certainly he was a good man!"

⁴⁸When the people who had gathered there to watch the spectacle saw what happened, they all went back home, beating their breasts. ⁴⁹All those who knew Jesus personally, including the women who had followed him from Galilee, stood off at a distance to see these things.

## The Burial of Jesus
(Also Matt. 27.57–61; Mark 15.42–47; John 19.38–42)

⁵⁰⁻⁵¹There was a man named Joseph, from the Jewish town of Arimathea. He was a good and honorable man, and waited for the coming of the Kingdom of God. Although a member of the Council, he had not agreed

with their decision and action. ⁵²He went into the presence of Pilate and asked for the body of Jesus. ⁵³Then he took the body down, wrapped it in a linen sheet, and placed it in a grave which had been dug out of the rock —a grave which had never been used. ⁵⁴It was Friday, and the Sabbath was about to begin.

⁵⁵The women who had followed Jesus from Galilee went with Joseph and saw the grave and how Jesus' body was placed in it. ⁵⁶Then they went back home and prepared the spices and ointments for his body.

On the Sabbath they rested, as the Law commanded.

## The Resurrection
*(Also Matt. 28,1–10; Mark 16.1–8; John 20.1–10)*

24 Very early on Sunday morning the women went to the grave carrying the spices they had prepared. ²They found the stone rolled away from the entrance to the grave, ³so they went in; but they did not find the body of the Lord Jesus. ⁴They stood there puzzled about this, when suddenly two men in bright shining clothes stood by them. ⁵Full of fear, the women bowed down to the ground, as the men said to them, "Why are you looking among the dead for one who is alive? ⁶He is not here; he has been raised. Remember what he said to you while he was in Galilee: ⁷'The Son of Man must be handed over to sinful men, be nailed to the cross, and rise to life on the third day.' "

*Told all these things*

⁸Then the women remembered his words, ⁹returned from the grave, and told all these things to the eleven

disciples and all the rest. [10]The women were Mary Magdalene, Joanna, and Mary the mother of James; they and the other women with them told these things to the apostles. [11]But the apostles thought that what the women said was nonsense, and did not believe them. [12]But Peter got up and ran to the grave; he bent down and saw the grave cloths and nothing else. Then he went back home wondering at what had happened.

## The Walk to Emmaus
(Also Mark 16.12–13)

[13]On that same day two of them were going to a village named Emmaus, about seven miles from Jerusalem, [14]and they were talking to each other about all the things that had happened. [15]As they talked and discussed, Jesus himself drew near and walked along with them; [16]they saw him, but somehow did not recognize him. [17]Jesus said to them, "What are you talking about, back and forth, as you walk along?"

They stood still, with sad faces. [18]One of them, named Cleopas, asked him, "Are you the only man living in Jerusalem who does not know what has been happening there these last few days?"

[19]"What things?" he asked.

"The things that happened to Jesus of Nazareth," they answered. "This man was a prophet, and was considered by God and by all the people to be mighty in words and deeds. [20]Our chief priests and rulers handed him over to be sentenced to death, and he was nailed to the cross. [21]And we had hoped that he would be the one who was going to redeem Israel! Besides all that, this is now the third day since it happened. [22]Some of the women of our group surprised us; they went at dawn to the grave, [23]but could not find his body. They came back saying they had seen a vision of angels who told them that he is alive. [24]Some of our group went to the grave and found it exactly as the women had said; but they did not see him."

[25]Then Jesus said to them, "How foolish you are, how slow you are to believe everything the prophets said! [26]Was it not necessary for the Messiah to suffer these things and enter his glory?" [27]And Jesus explained to them what was said about him in all the Scriptures,

beginning with the books of Moses and the writings of all the prophets.

²⁸They came near the village to which they were going, and Jesus acted as if he were going farther; ²⁹but they held him back, saying, "Stay with us; the day is almost over and it is getting dark." So he went in to stay with them. ³⁰He sat at table with them, took the bread, and said the blessing; then he broke the bread and gave it to them. ³¹Their eyes were opened and they recognized him; but he disappeared from their sight. ³²They said to each other, "Wasn't it like a fire burning in us when he talked to us on the road and explained the Scriptures to us?"

³³They got up at once and went back to Jerusalem, where they found the eleven disciples gathered together with the others ³⁴and saying, "The Lord is risen indeed! He has appeared to Simon!"

³⁵The two then explained to them what had happened on the road, and how they had recognized the Lord when he broke the bread.

## Jesus Appears to His Disciples
(Also Matt. 28.16–20; Mark 16.14–18; John 20.19–23; Acts 1.6–8)

³⁶While they were telling them this, suddenly the Lord himself stood among them and said to them, "Peace be with you."

³⁷Full of fear and terror, they thought that they were seeing a ghost. ³⁸But he said to them, "Why are you troubled? Why are these doubts coming up in your minds? ³⁹Look at my hands and my feet and see that it is I, myself. Feel me, and you will see, because a ghost doesn't have flesh and bones, as you can see I have."

⁴⁰He said this and showed them his hands and his feet. ⁴¹They still could not believe, they were so full of joy and wonder; so he asked them, "Do you have anything to eat here?" ⁴²They gave him a piece of cooked fish, ⁴³which he took and ate before them.

⁴⁴Then he said to them, "These are the very things I told you while I was still with you: everything written about me in the Law of Moses, the writings of the prophets, and the Psalms had to come true."

⁴⁵Then he opened their minds to understand the Scriptures, ⁴⁶and said to them, "This is what is written:

that the Messiah must suffer, and rise from death on the third day, [47]and that in his name the message about repentance and the forgiveness of sins must be preached to all nations, beginning in Jerusalem. [48]You are witnesses of these things. [49]And I myself will send upon you what my Father has promised. But you must wait in the city until the power from above comes down upon you."

## Jesus Is Taken up to Heaven
*(Also Mark 16.19–20; Acts 1.9–11)*

[50]Then he led them out of the city as far as Bethany, where he raised his hands and blessed them. [51]As he was blessing them, he departed from them and was taken up into heaven. [52]They worshiped him and went back into Jerusalem, filled with great joy, [53]and spent all their time in the temple giving thanks to God.

*He raised his hands and blessed them*

# THE ACTS OF THE APOSTLES

# THE ACTS OF THE APOSTLES

1 Dear Theophilus:
In my first book I wrote about all the things that Jesus did and taught, from the time he began his work [2]until the day he was taken up to heaven. Before he was taken up he gave instructions by the power of the Holy Spirit to the men he had chosen as his apostles. [3]For forty days after his death he showed himself to them many times, in ways that proved beyond doubt that he was alive; he was seen by them, and talked with them about the Kingdom of God. [4]And when they came together, he gave them this order, "Do not leave Jerusalem, but wait for the gift my Father promised, that I told you about. [5]John baptized with water, but in a few days you will be baptized with the Holy Spirit."

## Jesus Is Taken up to Heaven

[6]When the apostles met together with Jesus they asked him, "Lord, will you at this time give the Kingdom back to Israel?"

[7]Jesus said to them, "The times and occasions are set by my Father's own authority, and it is not for you to know when they will be. [8]But you will be filled with power when the Holy Spirit comes on you, and you will be witnesses for me in Jerusalem, in all of Judea and Samaria, and to the ends of the earth." [9]After saying this, he was taken up to heaven as they watched him; and a cloud hid him from their sight.

[10]They still had their eyes fixed on the sky as he went away, when two men dressed in white suddenly stood beside them. [11]"Men of Galilee," they said, "why do you stand there looking up at the sky? This Jesus, who was taken up from you into heaven, will come back in the same way that you saw him go to heaven."

## Judas' Successor

[12]Then the apostles went back to Jerusalem from the Mount of Olives, which is about half a mile away from the city. [13]They entered Jerusalem and went up to the

room where they were staying: Peter, John, James and
Andrew, Philip and Thomas, Bartholomew and Mat-
thew, James, the son of Alphaeus, Simon the Patriot,
and Judas, the son of James. ¹⁴They gathered frequently
to pray as a group, together with the women, and with
Mary the mother of Jesus, and his brothers.

¹⁵A few days later there was a meeting of the believers, about one hundred and twenty in all, and Peter
stood up to speak. ¹⁶"My brothers," he said, "the
scripture had to come true in which the Holy Spirit,
speaking through David, predicted about Judas, who
was the guide of those who arrested Jesus. ¹⁷Judas was
a member of our group, because he had been chosen to
have a part in our work."

¹⁸(With the money that Judas got for his evil act he
bought a field, where he fell to his death; he burst open
and all his insides spilled out. ¹⁹All the people living in
Jerusalem heard about it, and so in their own language
they call that field Akeldama, which means "Field of
Blood.")

²⁰"For it is written in the book of Psalms,
'May his house become empty;
    let no one live in it.'
It is also written,
'May someone else take his place of
    service.'

²¹⁻²²"So then, someone must join us as a witness to
the resurrection of the Lord Jesus. He must be one of
those who were in our group during the whole time
that the Lord Jesus traveled about with us, beginning
from the time John preached his baptism until the day
Jesus was taken up from us to heaven."

²³So they proposed two men: Joseph, who was called
Barsabbas (he was also called Justus), and Matthias.
²⁴Then they prayed, "Lord, you know the hearts of all
men. And so, Lord, show us which one of these two
you have chosen ²⁵to take this place of service as an
apostle which Judas left to go to the place where he
belongs." ²⁶Then they drew lots to choose between the
two names. The name chosen was that of Matthias,
and he was added to the group of the eleven apostles.

## The Coming of the Holy Spirit

2 When the day of Pentecost arrived, all the believers were gathered together in one place. [2]Suddenly there was a noise from the sky which sounded like a strong wind blowing, and it filled the whole house where they were sitting. [3]Then they saw what looked like tongues of fire spreading out; and each person there was touched by a tongue. [4]They were all filled with the Holy Spirit and began to talk in other languages, as the Spirit enabled them to speak.

[5]There were Jews living in Jerusalem, religious men who had come from every country in the world. [6]When they heard this noise, a large crowd gathered. They were all excited, because each one of them heard the believers talking in his own language. [7]In amazement and wonder they exclaimed, "These men who are talking like this—they are all Galileans! [8]How is it, then, that all of us hear them speaking in our own native language? [9]We are from Parthia, Media, and Elam; from Mesopotamia, Judea, and Cappadocia; from Pontus and Asia, [10]from Phrygia and Pamphylia, from Egypt and the regions of Libya near Cyrene; some of us are from Rome, [11]both Jews and Gentiles converted to Judaism; and some of us are from Crete and Arabia—yet all of us hear them speaking in our own languages of the great things that God has done!" [12]Amazed and confused they all kept asking each other, "What does this mean?"

[13]But others made fun of the believers, saying, "These men are drunk!"

## Peter's Message

[14]Then Peter stood up with the other eleven apostles, and in a loud voice began to speak to the crowd, "Fellow Jews, and all of you who live in Jerusalem, listen to me and let me tell you what this means. [15]These men are not drunk, as you suppose; it is only nine o'clock in the morning. [16]Rather, this is what the prophet Joel spoke about,

[17] 'This is what I will do in the last days, God says:

*Listen to me*

I will pour out my Spirit upon all men.
Your sons and your daughters will
prophesy;
your young men will see visions,
and your old men will dream dreams.
18 Yes, even on my slaves, both men and
women,
I will pour out my Spirit in those days,
and they will prophesy.
19 I will perform miracles in the sky above,
and marvels on the earth below.
There will be blood, fire, and thick smoke,
20 the sun will become dark,
and the moon red as blood,
before the great and glorious Day of the
Lord arrives.
21 And then, whoever calls on the name of
the Lord will be saved.'

22"Listen to these words, men of Israel! Jesus of
Nazareth was a man whose divine mission was clearly
shown to you by the miracles, wonders, and signs which

God did through him; you yourselves know this, for it took place here among you. ²³God, in his own will and knowledge, had already decided that Jesus would be handed over to you; and you killed him, by letting sinful men nail him to the cross. ²⁴But God raised him from the dead; he set him free from the pains of death, because it was impossible that death should hold him prisoner. ²⁵For David said about him,

> 'I saw the Lord before me at all times;
>> he is by my right side, so that I will not
>> be troubled.
> ²⁶ Because of this my heart is glad
>> and my words are full of joy;
> and I, mortal though I am,
>> will rest assured in hope,
> ²⁷ because you will not abandon my soul in
>> the world of the dead;
>> you will not allow your devoted servant
>> to suffer decay.
> ²⁸ You have shown me the paths that lead to
>> life,
>> and by your presence you will fill me
>> with joy.'

²⁹"Brothers: I must speak to you quite plainly about our patriarch David. He died and was buried, and his grave is here with us to this very day. ³⁰He was a prophet, and he knew God's promise to him: God made a vow that he would make one of David's descendants a king, just as David was. ³¹David saw what God was going to do, and so he spoke about the resurrection of the Messiah when he said,

> 'He was not abandoned in the world of the
>> dead;
>> his flesh did not decay.'

³²God has raised this very Jesus from the dead, and we are all witnesses to this fact. ³³He has been raised to the right side of God and received from him the Holy Spirit, as his Father had promised; and what you now see and hear is his gift that he has poured out on us. ³⁴For David himself did not go up into heaven; rather he said,

> 'The Lord said to my Lord:
>> Sit here at my right side,

<sup>35</sup> until I put your enemies as a footstool
   under your feet.'

<sup>36</sup>"All the people of Israel, then, are to know for sure
that it is this Jesus, whom you nailed to the cross, that
God has made Lord and Messiah!"

<sup>37</sup>When the people heard this, they were deeply
troubled, and said to Peter and the other apostles,
"What shall we do, brothers?"

<sup>38</sup>Peter said to them, "Turn away from your sins,
each one of you, and be baptized in the name of Jesus
Christ, so that your sins will be forgiven; and you will
receive God's gift, the Holy Spirit. <sup>39</sup>For God's promise was made to you and your children, and to all who
are far away—all whom the Lord our God calls to
himself."

<sup>40</sup>Peter made his appeal to them and with many
other words he urged them, saying, "Save yourselves
from the punishment coming to this wicked people!"
<sup>41</sup>Many of them believed his message and were bap-
tized; about three thousand people were added to the
group that day. <sup>42</sup>They spent their time in learning
from the apostles, taking part in the fellowship, and
sharing in the fellowship meals and the prayers.

### Life among the Believers

<sup>43</sup>Many miracles and wonders were done through the
apostles, and this caused everyone to be filled with awe.
<sup>44</sup>All the believers continued together in close fellow-
ship and shared their belongings with one another.
<sup>45</sup>They would sell their property and possessions and
distribute the money among all, according to what each
one needed. <sup>46</sup>Every day they continued to meet as a
group in the temple, and they had their meals together
in their homes, eating the food with glad and humble
hearts, <sup>47</sup>praising God, and enjoying the good will of all
the people. And every day the Lord added to their group
those who were being saved.

### The Lame Man Healed

3 One day Peter and John went to the temple at three
o'clock in the afternoon, the hour for prayers.
<sup>2</sup>There, at the "Beautiful Gate," as it was called, was a

*He looked at them, expecting to get something*

man who had been lame all his life. Every day he was carried to this gate to beg for money from the people who were going into the temple. ³When he saw Peter and John going in, he begged them to give him something. ⁴They looked straight at him and Peter said, "Look at us!" ⁵So he looked at them, expecting to get something from them. ⁶Peter said to him, "I have no money at all, but I will give you what I have: in the name of Jesus Christ of Nazareth I order you to walk!" ⁷Then he took him by his right hand and helped him up. At once the man's feet and ankles became strong; ⁸he jumped up, stood on his feet, and started walking around. Then he went into the temple with them, walking and jumping and praising God. ⁹The whole crowd saw him walking and praising God; ¹⁰and when they recognized him as the beggar who sat at the temple's "Beautiful Gate," they were all filled with surprise and amazement at what had happened to him.

## Peter's Message in the Temple

¹¹As the man held on to Peter and John, all the people were amazed and ran to them in "Solomon's Porch," as it was called. ¹²When Peter saw the people, he said to

them, "Men of Israel, why are you surprised at this, and
why do you stare at us? Do you think that it was by
means of our own power or godliness that we made this
man walk? [13]The God of Abraham, Isaac, and Jacob, the
God of our ancestors, has given divine glory to his Servant Jesus. You handed him over to the authorities, and
you rejected him in Pilate's presence, even after Pilate
had decided to set him free. [14]He was holy and good, but
you rejected him and instead you asked Pilate to do you
the favor of turning loose a murderer. [15]And so you
killed the one who leads men to life. But God raised him
from the dead—and we are witnesses to this. [16]It was the
power of his name that gave strength to this lame man.
What you see and know was done by faith in his name;
it was faith in Jesus that made him well like this before
you all.

[17]"And now, my brothers, I know that what you and
your leaders did to Jesus was done because of your
ignorance. [18]God long ago announced by means of all
the prophets that his Messiah had to suffer; and he
made it come true in this way. [19]Repent, then, and
turn to God, so that he will wipe away your sins, [20]so
that times of spiritual strength may come from the
Lord's presence, and that he may send Jesus, who is
the Messiah he has already chosen for you. [21]He must
remain in heaven until the time comes for all things to
be made new, as God announced by means of his holy
prophets of long ago. [22]For Moses said, 'The Lord
your God will send you a prophet, just as he sent me,
who will be of your own people. You must listen to
everything that he tells you. [23]Anyone who does not
listen to what that prophet says will be separated from
God's people and destroyed.' [24]And the prophets, including Samuel and those who came after him, all of
them who had a message, also announced these present days. [25]The promises of God through his prophets
are for you, and you share in the covenant which God
made with your ancestors. As he said to Abraham,
'Through your descendants I will bless all the people
on earth.' [26]And so God chose and sent his Servant to
you first, to bless you by making all of you turn away
from your wicked ways."

## Peter and John before the Council

4 Peter and John were still speaking to the people when the priests, the officer in charge of the temple guards, and the Sadducees came to them. ²They were annoyed because the two apostles were teaching the people that Jesus had risen from death, which proved that the dead will rise to life. ³So they arrested them and put them in jail until the next day, since it was already late. ⁴But many who heard the message believed; and the number of men came to about five thousand.

⁵The next day the Jewish leaders, the elders, and the teachers of the Law gathered in Jerusalem. ⁶They met with the High Priest Annas, and Caiaphas, and John, and Alexander, and the others who belonged to the High Priest's family. ⁷They made the apostles stand before them and asked them, "How did you do this? What power do you have, or whose name did you use?"

⁸Peter, full of the Holy Spirit, answered them, "Leaders of the people and elders: ⁹if we are being questioned today about the good deed done to the lame man and how he was made well, ¹⁰then you should all know, and all the people of Israel should know, that this man stands here before you completely well by the power of the name of Jesus Christ of Nazareth—whom you crucified and God raised from death. ¹¹Jesus is the one of whom the scripture says,

'The stone that you the builders despised
    turned out to be the most important
    stone.'

¹²Salvation is to be found through him alone; for there is no one else in all the world, whose name God has given to men, by whom we can be saved."

¹³The members of the Council were amazed to see how bold Peter and John were, and to learn that they were ordinary men of no education. They realized then that they had been companions of Jesus. ¹⁴But there was nothing that they could say, because they saw the man who had been made well standing there with Peter and John. ¹⁵So they told them to leave the Council room, and started discussing among themselves. ¹⁶"What shall we do with these men?" they asked.

"Everyone living in Jerusalem knows that this extraordinary miracle has been performed by them, and we cannot deny it. ¹⁷But to keep this matter from spreading any further among the people, let us warn these men never again to speak to anyone in the name of Jesus."

¹⁸So they called them back in and told them that under no condition were they to speak or to teach in the name of Jesus. ¹⁹But Peter and John answered them, "You yourselves judge which is right in God's sight, to obey you or to obey God. ²⁰For we cannot stop speaking of what we ourselves have seen and heard." ²¹The Council warned them even more strongly, and then set them free. They could find no reason for punishing them, because the people were all praising God for what had happened. ²²The man on whom this miracle of healing had been performed was over forty years old.

## The Believers Pray for Boldness

²³As soon as they were set free, Peter and John returned to their group and told them what the chief priests and the elders had said. ²⁴When they heard it, they all joined together in prayer to God: "Master and Creator of heaven, earth, and sea, and all that is in them! ²⁵By means of the Holy Spirit you spoke through our ancestor David, your servant, when he said,

'Why were the Gentiles furious;
    why did the peoples plot in vain?
²⁶ The kings of the earth prepared themselves,
    and the rulers met together
    against the Lord and his Messiah.'

²⁷For indeed Herod and Pontius Pilate met together in this city with the Gentiles and the people of Israel against Jesus, your holy Servant, whom you made Messiah. ²⁸They gathered to do everything that you, by your power and will, had already decided would take place. ²⁹And now, Lord, take notice of the threats they made and allow us, your servants, to speak your message with all boldness. ³⁰Stretch out your hand to heal, and grant that wonders and miracles may be performed through the name of your holy Servant Jesus."

³¹When they finished praying, the place where they were meeting was shaken. They were all filled with the Holy Spirit and began to speak God's message with boldness.

## All Things Together

³²The group of believers was one in mind and heart. No one said that any of his belongings was his own, but they all shared with one another everything they had. ³³With great power the apostles gave witness of the resurrection of the Lord Jesus, and God poured rich blessings on them all. ³⁴There was no one in the group who was in need. Those who owned fields or houses would sell them, bring the money received from the sale ³⁵and turn it over to the apostles; and the money was distributed to each one according to his need.

³⁶And so it was that Joseph, a Levite born in Cyprus, whom the apostles called Barnabas (which means "One who Encourages"), ³⁷sold a field he owned, brought the money, and turned it over to the apostles.

## Ananias and Sapphira

5 But there was a man named Ananias, whose wife was named Sapphira. He sold some property that belonged to them, ²but kept part of the money for himself, as his wife knew, and turned the rest over to the apostles. ³Peter said to him, "Ananias, why did you let Satan take control of your heart and make you lie to the Holy Spirit by keeping part of the money you received for the property? ⁴Before you sold the property it belonged to you, and after you sold it the money was yours. Why, then, did you decide in your heart that you would do such a thing? You have not lied to men—you have lied to God!" ⁵As soon as Ananias heard this he fell down dead; and all who heard about it were filled with fear. ⁶The young men came in, wrapped up his body, took him out, and buried him.

⁷About three hours later his wife came in, but she did not know what had happened. ⁸Peter said to her, "Tell me, was this the full amount you and your husband received for your property?"

"Yes," she answered, "the full amount."

⁹So Peter said to her, "Why did you and your husband decide to put the Lord's Spirit to the test? The men who buried your husband are at the door right now, and they will carry you out too!" ¹⁰At once she fell down at his feet and died. The young men came in and saw that she was dead, so they carried her out and buried her beside her husband. ¹¹The whole church and all the others who heard of this were filled with great fear.

## Miracles and Wonders

¹²Many miracles and wonders were being performed among the people by the apostles. All the believers met together in a group in Solomon's Porch. ¹³Nobody outside the group dared join them, even though the people spoke highly of them. ¹⁴But more and more people were added to the group—a crowd of men and women who believed in the Lord. ¹⁵As a result of what the apostles were doing, the sick people were carried out in the streets and placed on beds and mats so that, when Peter walked by, at least his shadow might fall on some of them. ¹⁶And crowds of people came in from the towns around Jerusalem, bringing their sick and those who had evil spirits in them; and they were all healed.

## The Apostles Persecuted

¹⁷Then the High Priest and all his companions, members of the local party of the Sadducees, became extremely jealous of the apostles; so they decided to take action. ¹⁸They arrested the apostles and placed them in the public jail. ¹⁹But that night an angel of the Lord opened the prison gates, led the apostles out, and said to them, ²⁰"Go and stand in the temple, and tell the people all about this new life." ²¹The apostles obeyed, and at dawn they entered the temple and started teaching.

The High Priest and his companions called together all the Jewish elders for a full meeting of the Council; then they sent orders to the prison to have the apostles brought before them. ²²But when the officials arrived, they did not find the apostles in prison; so they returned to the Council and reported, ²³"When we arrived at the jail we found it locked up tight and all the guards on

*Listen!*

watch at the gates; but when we opened the gates we did not find anyone inside!" ²⁴When the officer in charge of the temple guards and the chief priests heard this, they wondered what had happened to the apostles. ²⁵Then a man came in who said to them, "Listen! The men you put in prison are standing in the temple teaching the people!" ²⁶So the officer went off with his men and brought the apostles back. They did not use force, however, because they were afraid that the people might stone them.

²⁷They brought the apostles in and made them stand before the Council, and the High Priest questioned them. ²⁸"We gave you strict orders not to teach in the name of this man," he said; "but see what you have done! You have spread your teaching all over Jerusalem, and you want to make us responsible for his death!"

²⁹Peter and the other apostles answered back, "We must obey God, not men. ³⁰The God of our fathers raised Jesus from death, after you had killed him by nailing him to a cross. ³¹God raised him to his right side as Leader and Savior, to give to the people of Israel the opportunity to repent and have their sins forgiven. ³²We are witnesses to these things—we and the Holy Spirit, who is God's gift to those who obey him."

³³When the members of the Council heard this they were so furious that they decided to have the apostles put to death. ³⁴But one of them, a Pharisee named

Gamaliel, a teacher of the Law who was highly respected by all the people, stood up in the Council. He ordered the apostles to be taken out, ³⁵and then said to the Council, "Men of Israel, be careful what you are about to do to these men. ³⁶Some time ago Theudas appeared, claiming that he was somebody great; and about four hundred men joined him. But he was killed, all his followers were scattered, and his movement died out. ³⁷After this, Judas the Galilean appeared during the time of the census; he also drew a crowd after him, but he also was killed and all his followers were scattered. ³⁸And so in this case now, I tell you, do not take any action against these men. Leave them alone, because if this plan and work of theirs is a man-made thing, it will disappear; ³⁹but if it comes from God you cannot possibly defeat them. You could find yourselves fighting against God!"

The Council followed Gamaliel's advice. ⁴⁰They called the apostles in, had them whipped, and ordered them never again to speak in the name of Jesus; and then they set them free. ⁴¹The apostles left the Council, full of joy that God had considered them worthy to suffer disgrace for the name of Jesus. ⁴²And every day in the temple and in people's homes they continued to teach and preach the Good News about Jesus the Messiah.

## The Seven Helpers

6 Some time later, as the number of disciples kept growing, there was a quarrel between the Greek-speaking Jews and the native Jews. The Greek-speaking Jews said that their widows were being neglected in the daily distribution of funds. ²So the twelve apostles called the whole group of disciples together and said, "It is not right for us to neglect the preaching of God's word in order to handle finances. ³So then, brothers, choose seven men among you who are known to be full of the Holy Spirit and wisdom, and we will put them in charge of this matter. ⁴We ourselves, then, will give our full time to prayers and the work of preaching."

⁵The whole group was pleased with the apostles' proposal; so they chose Stephen, a man full of faith and

the Holy Spirit, and Philip, Prochorus, Nicanor, Timon, Parmenas, and Nicolaus, a Gentile from Antioch who had been converted to Judaism. ⁶The group presented them to the apostles, who prayed and placed their hands on them.

⁷And so the word of God continued to spread. The number of disciples in Jerusalem grew larger and larger, and a great number of priests accepted the faith.

### The Arrest of Stephen

⁸Stephen, a man richly blessed by God and full of power, performed great miracles and wonders among the people. ⁹But some men opposed him; they were members of the synagogue of the Free Men (as it was called), which had Jews from Cyrenia and Alexandria. They and other Jews from Cilicia and Asia started arguing with Stephen. ¹⁰But the Spirit gave Stephen such wisdom that when he spoke they could not resist him. ¹¹So they bribed some men to say, "We heard him speaking against Moses and against God!" ¹²In this way they stirred up the people, the elders, and the teachers of the Law. They came to Stephen, seized him, and took him before the Council. ¹³Then they brought in some men to tell lies about him. "This man," they said, "is always talking against our sacred temple and the Law of Moses. ¹⁴We heard him say that this Jesus of Nazareth will tear down the temple and change all the customs which have come down to us from Moses!" ¹⁵All those sitting in the Council fixed their eyes on Stephen and saw that his face looked like the face of an angel.

### Stephen's Speech

7 The High Priest asked Stephen, "Is this really so?" ²Stephen answered, "Brothers and fathers! Listen to me! The God of glory appeared to our ancestor Abraham while he was living in Mesopotamia, before he had gone to live in Haran, ³and said to him, 'Leave your family and country and go to the land that I will show you.' ⁴And so he left the land of Chaldea and went to live in Haran. After Abraham's father died, God made him move to this country, where you now live. ⁵God did not then give Abraham any part of it as his own, not even a square foot of ground; but God promised that he

would give it to him, and that it would belong to him and
his descendants after him. At the time God made this
promise Abraham had no children. ⁶This is what God
said to him, 'Your descendants will live in a foreign
country, where they will be slaves and will be badly
treated for four hundred years. ⁷But I will pass judgment
on the people that they will serve,' God said, 'and afterward they will come out of that country and will worship
me in this place.' ⁸Then God gave to Abraham the
ceremony of circumcision as a sign of the covenant. So
Abraham circumcised Isaac a week after he was born;
Isaac circumcised Jacob, and Jacob circumcised the
twelve patriarchs.

⁹"The patriarchs were jealous of Joseph, and sold
him to be a slave in Egypt. But God was with him,
¹⁰and brought him safely through all his troubles.
When Joseph appeared before Pharaoh, the king of
Egypt, God gave him a pleasing manner and wisdom.
Pharaoh made Joseph governor over the country and
the royal household. ¹¹Then there was a famine in all
of Egypt and Canaan, which caused much suffering.
Our ancestors could not find any food. ¹²So when
Jacob heard that there was grain in Egypt, he sent his
sons, our ancestors, on their first visit there. ¹³On the
second visit Joseph made himself known to his brothers, and Pharaoh came to know about Joseph's family.
¹⁴So Joseph sent a message to his father Jacob, telling
him and the whole family to come to Egypt; there
were seventy-five people in all. ¹⁵Then Jacob went
down to Egypt, where he and our ancestors died.
¹⁶Their bodies were moved to Shechem, where they
were buried in the grave which Abraham had bought
from the tribe of Hamor for a sum of money.

¹⁷"When the time drew near for God to keep the
promise he had made to Abraham, the number of our
people in Egypt had grown much larger. ¹⁸At last a
different king, who had not known Joseph, began to
rule in Egypt. ¹⁹He tricked our people and was cruel to
our ancestors, forcing them to put their babies out of
their homes, so that they would die. ²⁰It was at this
time that Moses was born, a very beautiful child. He
was brought up at home for three months, ²¹and when
he was put out of his home the daughter of Pharaoh

adopted him and brought him up as her own son. ²²He was taught all the wisdom of the Egyptians, and became a great man in words and deeds.

²³"When Moses was forty years old he decided to visit his fellow Israelites. ²⁴He saw one of them being mistreated by an Egyptian; so he went to his help and took revenge on the Egyptian by killing him. ²⁵(He thought that his own people would understand that God was going to use him to set them free; but they did not understand.) ²⁶The next day he saw two Israelites fighting, and he tried to make peace between them. 'Listen, men,' he said, 'you are brothers; why do you mistreat each other?' ²⁷But the one who was mistreating the other pushed Moses aside. 'Who made you ruler and judge over us?' he asked. ²⁸Do you want to kill me, just as you killed that Egyptian yesterday?' ²⁹When Moses heard this he fled from Egypt and started living in the land of Midian. There he had two sons.

³⁰"After forty years had passed, an angel appeared to Moses in the flames of a burning bush in the desert near Mount Sinai. ³¹Moses was amazed by what he saw, and went near the bush to look at it closely. But he heard the Lord's voice: ³²'I am the God of your ancestors, the God of Abraham, Isaac, and Jacob.' Moses trembled with fear and dared not look. ³³The Lord said to him, 'Take your sandals off, for the place where you are standing is holy ground. ³⁴I have looked and seen the cruel suffering of my people in Egypt. I have heard their groans, and I have come down to save them. Come now, I will send you to Egypt.'

³⁵"Moses is the one who was rejected by the people of Israel. 'Who made you ruler and judge over us?' they asked. He is the one whom God sent as ruler and savior, with the help of the angel who appeared to him in the burning bush. ³⁶He led the people out of Egypt, performing miracles and wonders in Egypt and the Red Sea, and in the desert for forty years. ³⁷Moses is the one who said to the people of Israel, 'God will send you a prophet, just as he sent me, who will be of your own people.' ³⁸He is the one who was with the people of Israel assembled in the desert; he was there with our ancestors and with the angel who spoke to

him on Mount Sinai; he received God's living messages to pass on to us.

<sup>39</sup>"But our ancestors refused to obey him; they pushed him aside and wished that they could go back to Egypt. <sup>40</sup>So they said to Aaron, 'Make us some gods who will go in front of us. We do not know what has happened to that Moses who brought us out of Egypt.' <sup>41</sup>It was then that they made an idol in the shape of a calf, offered sacrifice to it, and had a feast to celebrate what they themselves had made. <sup>42</sup>But God turned away from them, and gave them over to worship the stars of heaven, as it is written in the book of the prophets,

> 'People of Israel! It was not to me
> > that you slaughtered and sacrificed animals
> > for forty years in the desert.
> <sup>43</sup> It was the tent of the god Moloch that you carried,
> > and the image of the star of your god Rephan;
> > they were idols that you had made to worship.
> And so I will send you away beyond Babylon.'

<sup>44</sup>"Our ancestors had the tent of God's presence with them in the desert. It had been made as God had told Moses to make it, according to the pattern that Moses had been shown. <sup>45</sup>Later on, our ancestors who received the tent from their fathers carried it with them when they went with Joshua and took over the land from the nations that God drove out before them. And it stayed there until the time of David. <sup>46</sup>He won God's favor, and asked God to allow him to provide a house for the God of Jacob. <sup>47</sup>But it was Solomon who built him a house.

<sup>48</sup>"But the Most High God does not live in houses built by men; as the prophet says,

> <sup>49</sup> 'Heaven is my throne, says the Lord,
> > and earth is my footstool.
> What kind of house would you build for me?
> Where is the place for me to rest?

$^{50}$ Did not I myself make all these things?"

$^{51}$"How stubborn you are! How heathen your hearts, how deaf you are to God's message! You are just like your ancestors: you too have always resisted the Holy Spirit! $^{52}$Was there any prophet that your ancestors did not persecute? They killed God's messengers, who long ago announced the coming of his righteous Servant. And now you have betrayed and murdered him. $^{53}$You are the ones who received God's law, that was handed down by angels—yet you have not obeyed it!"

### The Stoning of Stephen

$^{54}$As the members of the Council listened to Stephen they became furious and ground their teeth at him in anger. $^{55}$But Stephen, full of the Holy Spirit, looked up to heaven and saw God's glory, and Jesus standing at the right side of God. $^{56}$"Look!" he said. "I see heaven opened and the Son of Man standing at the right side of God!"

*They threw him out of the city and stoned him*

<sup>57</sup>With a loud cry they covered their ears with their hands. Then they all rushed together at him at once, <sup>58</sup>threw him out of the city and stoned him. The witnesses left their cloaks in charge of a young man named Saul. <sup>59</sup>They kept on stoning Stephen as he called on the Lord, "Lord Jesus, receive my spirit!" <sup>60</sup>He knelt down and cried out in a loud voice, "Lord! Do not remember this sin against them!" He said this and died.

8 And Saul approved of his murder.

## Saul Persecutes the Church

That very day the church in Jerusalem began to suffer cruel persecution. All the believers, except the apostles, were scattered throughout the provinces of Judea and Samaria. <sup>2</sup>Some devout men buried Stephen, mourning for him with loud cries.

<sup>3</sup>But Saul tried to destroy the church; going from house to house, he dragged out the believers, both men and women, and threw them into jail.

## The Gospel Preached in Samaria

<sup>4</sup>The believers who were scattered went everywhere, preaching the message. <sup>5</sup>Philip went to the city of Samaria and preached the Messiah to the people there. <sup>6</sup>The crowds paid close attention to what Philip said. They all listened to him and saw the miracles that he performed. <sup>7</sup>Evil spirits came out with a loud cry from many people; many paralyzed and lame people were also healed. <sup>8</sup>So there was great joy in Samaria.

<sup>9</sup>In that city lived a man named Simon, who for some time had astounded the Samaritans with his magic. He claimed that he was someone great, <sup>10</sup>and everyone in the city, from all classes of society, paid close attention to him. "He is that power of God known as 'The Great Power,' " they said. <sup>11</sup>He had astounded them with his magic for such a long time that they paid close attention to him. <sup>12</sup>But when they believed Philip's message about the Good News of the Kingdom of God and the name of Jesus Christ, they were baptized, both men and women. <sup>13</sup>Simon himself also believed; and after being baptized he stayed close to Philip, and was astounded when he saw the great wonders and miracles that were being performed.

¹⁴The apostles in Jerusalem heard that the people of Samaria had received the word of God; so they sent Peter and John to them. ¹⁵When they arrived, they prayed for the believers that they might receive the Holy Spirit. ¹⁶For the Holy Spirit had not yet come down on any of them; they had only been baptized in the name of the Lord Jesus. ¹⁷Then Peter and John placed their hands on them, and they received the Holy Spirit.

¹⁸Simon saw that the Spirit had been given to them when the apostles placed their hands on them. So he offered money to Peter and John, ¹⁹and said, "Give this power to me too, so that anyone I place my hands on will receive the Holy Spirit."

²⁰But Peter answered him, "May you and your money go to hell, for thinking that you can buy God's gift with money! ²¹You have no part or share in our work, because your heart is not right in God's sight. ²²Repent, then, from this evil plan of yours, and pray to the Lord that he will forgive you for thinking such a thing as this. ²³For I see that you are full of bitter envy, and are a prisoner of sin."

²⁴Simon said to Peter and John, "Please pray to the Lord for me, so that none of these things you said will happen to me."

²⁵After they had given their testimony and spoken the Lord's message, Peter and John went back to Jerusalem. On their way they preached the Good News in many villages of Samaria.

## Philip and the Ethiopian Official

²⁶An angel of the Lord spoke to Philip, "Get yourself ready and go south to the road that goes from Jerusalem to Gaza." (This road is no longer used.) ²⁷⁻²⁸So Philip got ready and went. Now an Ethiopian eunuch was on his way home. This man was an important official in charge of the treasury of the Queen, or Candace, of Ethiopia. He had been to Jerusalem to worship God, and was going back in his carriage. As he rode along he was reading from the book of the prophet Isaiah. ²⁹The Holy Spirit said to Philip, "Go over and stay close to that carriage." ³⁰Philip ran over and heard him reading

from the book of the prophet Isaiah; so he asked him, "Do you understand what you are reading?"

[31] "How can I understand," the official replied, "unless someone explains it to me?" And he invited Philip to climb up and sit in the carriage with him. [32] The passage of scripture which he was reading was this,

> "He was like a sheep that is taken to be
>     slaughtered;
> he was like a lamb that makes no
>     sound when its wool is cut off;
> he did not say a word.
> [33] He was humiliated, and justice was de-
>     nied him.
> No one will be able to tell about his de-
>     scendants,
>     because his life on earth has come to
>     an end."

[34] The official said to Philip, "Tell me, of whom is the prophet saying this? Of himself or of someone else?" [35] Philip began to speak; starting from this very passage of scripture, he told him the Good News about Jesus. [36] As they traveled down the road they came to a place where there was some water, and the official said, ":Here is some water. What is to keep me from being baptized?"

[ [37] Philip said to him, "You may be baptized if you believe with all your heart."

"I do," he answered; "I believe that Jesus Christ is the Son of God." ]

[38] The official ordered the carriage to stop; and both of them, Philip and the official, went down into the water, and Philip baptized him. [39] When they came up out of the water the Spirit of the Lord took Philip away. The official did not see him again, but continued on his way, full of joy. [40] Philip found himself in Ashdod; and he went through all the towns preaching the Good News, until he arrived at Caesarea.

### The Conversion of Saul
(Also Acts 22.6–16; 26.12–18)

9 In the meantime Saul kept up his violent threats of murder against the disciples of the Lord. He went to the High Priest [2] and asked for letters of introduction

to the Jewish synagogues in Damascus, so that if he should find any followers of the Way of the Lord there, he would be able to arrest them, both men and women, and take them back to Jerusalem.

*He fell to the ground*

³On his way to Damascus, as he came near the city, suddenly a light from the sky flashed around him. ⁴He fell to the ground and heard a voice saying to him, "Saul, Saul! Why do you persecute me?"

⁵"Who are you, Lord?" he asked.

"I am Jesus, whom you persecute," the voice said. ⁶"But get up and go into the city, where you will be told what you must do."

⁷The men who were traveling with Saul had stopped, not saying a word; they heard the voice but could not see anyone. ⁸Saul got up from the ground and opened his eyes, but could not see a thing. So they took him by the hand and led him into Damascus. ⁹For three

days he was not able to see, and during that time he did not eat or drink anything.

¹⁰There was a disciple in Damascus named Ananias. He had a vision, in which the Lord said to him, "Ananias!"

"Here I am, Lord," he answered.

¹¹The Lord said to him, "Get ready and go to Straight Street, and at the house of Judas ask for a man from Tarsus named Saul. He is praying, ¹²and in a vision he saw a man named Ananias come in and place his hands on him so that he might see again."

¹³Ananias answered, "Lord, many people have told me about this man, about all the terrible things he has done to your people in Jerusalem. ¹⁴And he has come to Damascus with authority from the chief priests to arrest all who call on your name."

¹⁵The Lord said to him, "Go, because I have chosen him to serve me, to make my name known to Gentiles and kings, and to the people of Israel. ¹⁶And I myself will show him all that he must suffer for my sake."

¹⁷So Ananias went, entered the house, and placed his hands on Saul. "Brother Saul," he said, "the Lord has sent me—Jesus himself, who appeared to you on the road as you were coming here. He sent me so that you might see again and be filled with the Holy Spirit." ¹⁸At once something like fish scales fell from Saul's eyes and he was able to see again. He stood up and was baptized; ¹⁹and after he had eaten, his strength came back.

### Saul Preaches in Damascus

Saul stayed for a few days with the disciples in Damascus. ²⁰He went straight to the synagogues and began to preach about Jesus. "He is the Son of God," he said.

²¹All who heard him were amazed, and asked, "Isn't this the man who in Jerusalem was killing those who call on this name? And didn't he come here for the very purpose of arresting them and taking them back to the chief priests?"

²²But Saul's preaching became even more powerful, and his proofs that Jesus was the Messiah were so con-

vincing that the Jews who lived in Damascus could not
answer him.

²³After many days had gone by, the Jews gathered
and made plans to kill Saul; ²⁴but he was told of what
they planned to do. Day and night they watched the
city gates in order to kill him. ²⁵But one night Saul's
followers took him and let him down through an opening in the wall, lowering him in a basket.

## Saul in Jerusalem

²⁶Saul went to Jerusalem and tried to join the disciples. They would not believe, however, that he was a
disciple, and they were all afraid of him. ²⁷Then Barnabas came to his help and took him to the apostles. He
explained to them how Saul had seen the Lord on the
road, and that the Lord had spoken to him. He also told
them how boldly Saul had preached in the name of Jesus
in Damascus. ²⁸And so Saul stayed with them and went
all over Jerusalem, preaching boldly in the name of the
Lord. ²⁹He also talked and disputed with the Greek-
speaking Jews, but they tried to kill him. ³⁰When the
brothers found out about this, they took Saul down to
Caesarea and sent him away to Tarsus.

³¹And so it was that the church throughout all of
Judea, Galilee, and Samaria had a time of peace. It was
built up and grew in numbers through the help of the
Holy Spirit, as it lived in reverence for the Lord.

## Peter in Lydda and Joppa

³²Peter traveled everywhere, and one time he went to
visit God's people who lived in Lydda. ³³There he met
a man named Aeneas, who was paralyzed and had not
been able to get out of bed for eight years. ³⁴"Aeneas,"
Peter said to him, "Jesus Christ makes you well. Get up
and make your bed." At once Aeneas got up. ³⁵All the
people living in Lydda and Sharon saw him, and they
turned to the Lord.

³⁶In Joppa there was a woman named Tabitha, who
was a believer. (Her name in Greek is Dorcas, meaning
a deer.) She spent all her time doing good and helping
the poor. ³⁷At that time she got sick and died. Her body

was washed and laid in a room upstairs. ³⁸Joppa was not very far from Lydda, and when the disciples in Joppa heard that Peter was in Lydda, they sent two men to him with the message, "Please hurry and come to us." ³⁹So Peter got ready and went with them. When he arrived he was taken to the room upstairs. All the widows crowded around him, crying and showing him the shirts and coats that Dorcas had made while she was alive. ⁴⁰Peter put them all out of the room, and knelt down and prayed; then he turned to the body and said, "Tabitha, get up!" She opened her eyes, and when she saw Peter she sat up. ⁴¹Peter reached over and helped her get up. Then he called the believers and the widows, and presented her alive to them. ⁴²The news about this spread all over Joppa, and many people believed in the Lord. ⁴³Peter stayed on in Joppa for many days with a leatherworker named Simon.

## Peter and Cornelius

**10** There was a man in Caesarea named Cornelius, a captain in the Roman army regiment called "The Italian Regiment." ²He was a religious man; he and his whole family worshiped God. He did much to help the Jewish poor people, and was constantly praying to God. ³It was about three o'clock one afternoon when he had a vision, in which he clearly saw an angel of God come in and say to him, "Cornelius!"

⁴He stared at the angel in fear and said, "What is it, sir?"

The angel answered, "God has accepted your prayers and works of charity, and has remembered you. ⁵And now send some men to Joppa to call for a certain man whose full name is Simon Peter. ⁶He is a guest in the home of a leatherworker named Simon, who lives by the sea." ⁷Then the angel who was speaking to him went away, and Cornelius called two of his house servants and a soldier, a religious man who was one of his personal attendants. ⁸He told them what had happened and sent them off to Joppa.

⁹The next day, as they were on their way and coming near Joppa, Peter went up on the roof of the house about noon in order to pray. ¹⁰He became hungry, and wanted

to eat; while the food was being prepared he had a vision. ¹¹He saw heaven opened and something coming down that looked like a large sheet being lowered by its four corners to the earth. ¹²In it were all kinds of animals, reptiles, and wild birds. ¹³A voice said to him, "Get up, Peter; kill and eat!"

¹⁴But Peter said, "Certainly not, Lord! I have never eaten anything considered defiled or unclean."

¹⁵The voice spoke to him again, "Do not consider anything unclean that God has declared clean." ¹⁶This happened three times; and then the thing was taken back up into heaven.

¹⁷Peter was wondering about the meaning of this vision that he had seen. In the meantime the men sent by Cornelius had learned where Simon's house was, and were now standing in front of the gate. ¹⁸They called out and asked, "Is there a guest here by the name of Simon Peter?"

¹⁹Peter was still trying to understand what the vision meant, when the Spirit said, "Listen! Three men are here looking for you. ²⁰So get yourself ready and go down, and do not hesitate to go with them, because I have sent them." ²¹So Peter went down and said to the men, "I am the man you are looking for. Why have you come?"

²²"Captain Cornelius sent us," they answered. "He is a good man who worships God and is highly respected by all the Jewish people. He was told by one of God's angels to invite you to his house, so that he could hear what you have to say." ²³Peter invited the men in and had them spend the night there.

The next day he got ready and went with them; and some of the brothers from Joppa went along with him. ²⁴The following day he arrived in Caesarea, where Cornelius was waiting for him, together with relatives and close friends that he had invited. ²⁵As Peter was about to go in, Cornelius met him, fell at his feet, and bowed down before him. ²⁶But Peter made him rise. "Stand up," he said, "because I myself am only a man." ²⁷Peter kept on talking to Cornelius as he went into the house, where he found many people gathered. ²⁸He said to them, "You yourselves know very well

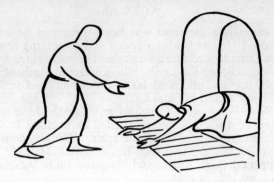

*"Stand up," he said, "because I myself am only a man"*

that a Jew is not allowed by his religion to visit or associate with a Gentile. But God has shown me that I must not consider any man unclean or defiled. ²⁹And so when you sent for me I came without any objection. I ask you, then, why did you send for me?"

³⁰Cornelius said, "It was about this time three days ago that I was praying in my house at three o'clock in the afternoon. Suddenly a man dressed in shining clothes stood in front of me ³¹and said: 'Cornelius! God has heard your prayer, and has remembered your works of charity. ³²Send someone to Joppa to call for a man whose full name is Simon Peter. He is a guest in the home of Simon the leatherworker, who lives by the sea.' ³³And so I sent for you at once, and you have been good enough to come. Now we are all here in the presence of God, waiting to hear anything that the Lord has ordered you to say."

## Peter's Speech

³⁴Peter began to speak: "I now realize that it is true that God treats all men on the same basis. ³⁵Whoever fears him and does what is right is acceptable to him, no matter what race he belongs to. ³⁶You know the message he sent to the people of Israel, proclaiming the Good News of peace through Jesus Christ, who is Lord of all men. ³⁷You know of the great event that took place throughout all the land of Israel, beginning in Galilee, after the baptism that John preached. ³⁸You know about

Jesus of Nazareth, how God poured out on him the Holy Spirit and power. He went everywhere, doing good and healing all who were under the power of the Devil, because God was with him. [39]We are witnesses of all that he did in the country of the Jews and in Jerusalem. They put him to death by nailing him to the cross. [40]But God raised him from death on the third day, and caused him to appear, [41]not to all the people, but only to us who are the witnesses that God had already chosen. We ate and drank with him after he rose from death. [42]And he commanded us to preach the gospel to the people, and to testify that he is the one whom God has appointed judge of the living and the dead. [43]All the prophets spoke about him, saying that everyone who believes in him will have his sins forgiven through the power of his name."

### The Gentiles Receive the Holy Spirit

[44]While Peter was still speaking, the Holy Spirit came down on all those who were listening to the message. [45]The Jewish believers who had come from Joppa with Peter were amazed that God had poured out his gift of the Holy Spirit on the Gentiles also. [46]For they heard them speaking in strange tongues and praising God's greatness. Peter spoke up, [47]"These people have received the Holy Spirit, just as we also did. Can anyone, then, stop them from being baptized with water?" [48]So he ordered them to be baptized in the name of Jesus Christ. Then they asked him to stay with them for a few days.

### Peter's Report to the Church at Jerusalem

**11** The apostles and the brothers throughout all of Judea heard that the Gentiles also had received the word of God. [2]When Peter went up to Jerusalem, those who were in favor of circumcising Gentiles criticized him, [3]"You were a guest in the home of uncircumcised Gentiles, and you even ate with them!" [4]So Peter gave them a full account of what had happened, from the very beginning:
[5]"I was praying in the city of Joppa, and I had a vision. I saw something coming down that looked like a large

sheet being lowered by its four corners from heaven, and it stopped next to me. [6]I looked closely inside and saw animals, beasts, reptiles, and wild birds. [7]Then I heard a voice saying to me, 'Get up, Peter; kill and eat!' [8]But I said, 'Certainly not, Lord! No defiled or unclean food has ever entered my mouth.' [9]The voice spoke again from heaven, 'Do not consider anything unclean that God has declared clean.' [10]This happened three times, and finally the whole thing was drawn back up into heaven. [11]At that very moment three men who had been sent to me from Caesarea arrived at the house where I was staying. [12]The Spirit told me to go with them without hesitation.These six brothers from Joppa also went with me to Caesarea, and we all went into the house of Cornelius. [13]He told us how he had seen an angel standing in his house who said to him, 'Send someone to Joppa to call for a man whose full name is Simon Peter. [14]He will speak words to you by which you and all your family will be saved.' [15]And when I began to speak, the Holy Spirit came down on them just as on us at the beginning. [16]Then I remembered what the Lord had said, 'John baptized with water, but you will be baptized with the Holy Spirit.' [17]It is clear that God gave those Gentiles the same gift that he gave us when we believed in the Lord Jesus Christ; who was I, then, to try to stop God!"

[18]When they heard this, they stopped their criticism and praised God, saying, "Then God has given to the Gentiles also the opportunity to repent and live!"

### The Church at Antioch

[19]The believers were scattered by the persecution which took place when Stephen was killed. Some of them went as far as Phoenicia and Cyprus and Antioch, telling the message to Jews only. [20]But some of the believers, men from Cyprus and Cyrene, went to Antioch and proclaimed the message to Gentiles also, telling them the Good News about the Lord Jesus. [21]The Lord's power was with them, and a great number of people believed and turned to the Lord.

[22]The news about this reached the church in Jerusalem, so they sent Barnabas to Antioch. [23]When he ar-

rived and saw how God had blessed the people, he was glad and urged them all to be faithful and true to the Lord with all their hearts. ²⁴Barnabas was a good man, full of the Holy Spirit and faith. Many people were brought to the Lord.

²⁵Then Barnabas went to Tarsus to look for Saul. ²⁶When he found him, he brought him to Antioch. For a whole year the two met with the people of the church and taught a large group. It was at Antioch that the disciples were first called Christians.

²⁷About that time some prophets went down from Jerusalem to Antioch. ²⁸One of them, named Agabus, stood up and by the power of the Spirit predicted that a great famine was about to come over all the earth. (It came when Claudius was Emperor.) ²⁹The disciples decided that each of them would send as much as he could to help their brothers who lived in Judea. ³⁰They did this, then, and sent the money to the church elders by Barnabas and Saul.

## More Persecution

12 About this time King Herod began to persecute some members of the church. ²He had James, the brother of John, put to death by the sword. ³When he saw that this pleased the Jews, he went ahead and had Peter arrested. (This happened during the time of the Feast of Unleavened Bread.) ⁴After his arrest Peter was put in jail, where he was handed over to be guarded by four groups of four soldiers each. Herod planned to put him on trial in public after Passover. ⁵So Peter was kept in jail, but the people of the church were praying earnestly to God for him.

## Peter Set Free from Prison

⁶The night before Herod was going to bring him out to the people, Peter was sleeping between two guards. He was tied with two chains, and there were guards on duty at the prison gate. ⁷Suddenly an angel of the Lord stood there, and a light shone in the cell. The angel shook Peter by the shoulder, woke him up, and said, "Hurry! Get up!" At once the chains fell off Peter's hands. ⁸Then the angel said, "Tighten your belt and tie

*Peter was sleeping between two guards*

on your sandals." Peter did so, and the angel said, "Put your cloak around you and come with me." ⁹Peter followed him out of the prison. He did not know, however, if what the angel was doing was real; he thought he was seeing a vision. ¹⁰They passed by the first guard station, and then the second, and came at last to the iron gate that opens into the city. The gate opened for them by itself, and they went out. They walked down a street, and suddenly the angel left Peter.

¹¹Then Peter realized what had happened to him, and said, "Now I know that it is really true! The Lord sent his angel, and he rescued me from Herod's power and from all the things the Jewish people expected to do."

¹²Aware of his situation, he went to the home of Mary, the mother of John Mark. Many people had gathered there and were praying. ¹³Peter knocked at the outside door, and a servant girl named Rhoda came to answer it. ¹⁴She recognized Peter's voice and was so happy that she ran back in without opening the door, and announced that Peter was standing outside. ¹⁵"You are crazy!" they told her. But she insisted that it was true. So they answered, "It is his angel."

[16]Meanwhile, Peter kept on knocking. They opened the door at last and when they saw him they were amazed. [17]He motioned with his hand for them to be quiet, and explained to them how the Lord had brought him out of prison. "Tell this to James and the rest of the brothers," he said; then he left and went somewhere else.

[18]When morning came, there was a tremendous confusion among the guards; what had happened to Peter? [19]Herod gave orders to search for him, but they could not find him. So he had the guards questioned and ordered them to be put to death.

After this Herod went down from Judea and spent some time in Caesarea.

## The Death of Herod

[20]Herod was very angry with the people of Tyre and Sidon; so they went in a group to see Herod. First they won Blastus over to their side; he was in charge of the palace. Then they went to Herod and asked him for peace, because their country got its food supplies from the king's country.

[21]On a chosen day Herod put on his royal robes, sat on his throne, and made a speech to the people. [22]"It isn't a man speaking, but a god!" they shouted. [23]At once the angel of the Lord struck Herod down, because he did not give honor to God. He was eaten by worms and died.

[24]The word of God continued to spread and grow.

[25]Barnabas and Saul finished their mission and returned from Jerusalem, taking John Mark with them.

## Barnabas and Saul Chosen and Sent

13 In the church at Antioch there were some prophets and teachers: Barnabas, Simeon (called the Black), Lucius (from Cyrene), Manaen (who had been brought up with Governor Herod), and Saul. [2]While they were serving the Lord and fasting, the Holy Spirit said to them, "Set apart for me Barnabas and Saul, to do the work to which I have called them."

[3]They fasted and prayed, placed their hands on them, and sent them off.

### In Cyprus

⁴Barnabas and Saul, then, having been sent by the Holy Spirit, went down to Seleucia and sailed from there to the island of Cyprus. ⁵When they arrived at Salamis, they preached the word of God in the Jewish synagogues. They had John Mark with them to help in the work.

⁶They went all the way across the island to Paphos, where they met a certain magician named Bar-Jesus, a Jew who claimed to be a prophet. ⁷He was a friend of the Governor of the island, Sergius Paulus, who was an intelligent man. The Governor called Barnabas and Saul before him because he wanted to hear the word of God. ⁸But they were opposed by the magician Elymas (this is his name in Greek); he tried to turn the Governor away from the faith. ⁹Then Saul—also known as Paul—was filled with the Holy Spirit; he looked straight at the magician ¹⁰and said, "You son of the Devil! You are the enemy of everything that is good; you are full of all kinds of evil tricks, and you always keep trying to turn the Lord's truths into lies! ¹¹The Lord's hand will come down on you now; you will be blind, and will not see the light of day for a time."

At once Elymas felt a black mist cover his eyes, and he walked around trying to find someone to lead him by the hand. ¹²The Governor believed when he saw what had happened; he was greatly amazed at the teaching about the Lord.

### In Antioch of Pisidia

¹³Paul and his companions sailed from Paphos and came to Perga, in Pamphylia; but John Mark left them there and went back to Jerusalem. ¹⁴They went on from Perga and came to Antioch of Pisidia; and on the Sabbath day they went into the synagogue and sat down. ¹⁵After the reading from the Law of Moses and the writings of the prophets, the officials of the synagogue sent them a message: "Brothers, we want you to speak to the people if you have a message of encouragement for them." ¹⁶Paul stood up, motioned with his hand, ·and began to speak:

"Fellow Israelites and all Gentiles here who worship

God: hear me! [17]The God of this people of Israel chose our ancestors, and made the people a great nation during the time they lived as foreigners in the land of Egypt. God brought them out of Egypt by his great power, [18]and for forty years he endured them in the desert. [19]He destroyed seven nations in the land of Canaan and made his people the owners of the land [20]for about four hundred and fifty years.

"After this he gave them judges, until the time of the prophet Samuel. [21]And when they asked for a king, God gave them Saul, the son of Kish, from the tribe of Benjamin, to be their king for forty years. [22]After removing him, God made David their king. This is what God said about him, 'I have found that David, the son of Jesse, is the kind of man I like, a man who will do all I want him to do.' [23]It was Jesus, a descendant of David, that God made the Savior of the people of Israel, as he had promised. [24]Before Jesus began his work, John preached to all the people of Israel that they should turn from their sins and be baptized. [25]And as John was about to finish his mission, he said to the people, 'Who do you think I am? I am not the one you are waiting for. But look! He is coming after me, and I am not good enough to take his sandals off his feet.'

[26]"My brothers, descendants of Abraham, and all Gentiles here who worship God: it is to us that this message of salvation has been sent! [27]For the people who live in Jerusalem, and their leaders, did not know that he is the Savior, nor did they understand the words of the prophets that are read every Sabbath day. Yet they made the prophets' words come true by condemning Jesus. [28]And even though they could find no reason to pass the death sentence on him, they asked Pilate to have him put to death. [29]And after they had done everything that the Scriptures say about him, they took him down from the cross and placed him in a grave. [30]But God raised him from the dead, [31]and for many days he appeared to those who had traveled with him from Galilee to Jerusalem. They are now witnesses for him to the people of Israel. [32-33]And we are here to bring the Good News to you: what God promised our ancestors he would do, he has now done for

us, who are their descendants, by raising Jesus to life.
As it is written in the second Psalm,

'You are my Son;
today I have become your Father.'

³⁴And this is what God said about raising him from the
dead, never again to return to decay,

'I will give you the sacred and sure blessings
that I promised to David.'

³⁵As indeed he says in another passage,

'You will not allow your devoted servant
to suffer decay.'

³⁶For David served God's purposes in his own time;
and then he died, was buried beside his ancestors, and
suffered decay. ³⁷But the one whom God raised from
the dead did not suffer decay. ³⁸⁻³⁹All of you, my
brothers, are to know for sure that it is through Jesus
that the message about forgiveness of sins is preached
to you; you are to know that everyone who believes in
him is set free from all the sins from which the Law of
Moses could not set you free. ⁴⁰Take care, then, so
that what the prophets said may not happen to you,

⁴¹'Look, you scoffers! Wonder and die!
For the work that I am doing in your
own day
is something that you will not believe,
even when someone explains it to
you!' "

⁴²As Paul and Barnabas were leaving the synagogue,
the people invited them to come back the next Sabbath
and tell them more about these things. ⁴³After the people had left the meeting, Paul and Barnabas were followed by many Jews and many Gentiles converted to
Judaism. The apostles spoke to them and encouraged
them to keep on living in the grace of God.

⁴⁴The next Sabbath day nearly everyone in the town
came to hear the word of the Lord. ⁴⁵When the Jews
saw the crowds, they were filled with jealousy; they
spoke against what Paul was saying and insulted him.
⁴⁶But Paul and Barnabas spoke out even more boldly,
"It was necessary that the word of God should be
spoken first to you. But since you reject it, and do not
consider yourselves worthy of eternal life, we will

leave you and go to the Gentiles. ⁴⁷For this is the commandment that the Lord has given us,

'I have set you to be a light for the
  Gentiles,
    to be the way of salvation for the
      whole world.' "

⁴⁸When the Gentiles heard this they were glad and praised the Lord's message; and those who had been chosen for eternal life became believers.

*Shook the dust off their feet against them*

⁴⁹The word of the Lord spread everywhere in that region. ⁵⁰But the Jews stirred up the leading men of the city and the Gentile women of high social standing who worshiped God. They started a persecution against Paul and Barnabas, and threw them out of their region. ⁵¹The apostles shook the dust off their feet against them and went on to Iconium. ⁵²The disciples in Antioch were full of joy and the Holy Spirit.

### In Iconium

**14** The same thing happened in Iconium: Paul and Barnabas went to the Jewish synagogue and

spoke in such a way that a great number of Jews and
Gentiles became believers. [2]But the Jews who would not
believe stirred up the Gentiles and turned their feelings
against the brothers. [3]The apostles stayed there for a
long time. They spoke boldly about the Lord, who
proved that their message about his grace was true by
giving them the power to perform miracles and wonders. [4]The crowd in the city was divided: some were for
the Jews, others for the apostles.

[5]Then the Gentiles and the Jews, together with their
leaders, decided to mistreat the apostles and stone
them. [6]When the apostles learned about it they fled to
Lystra and Derbe, cities in Lycaonia, and to the surrounding territory. [7]There they preached the Good
News.

### In Lystra and Derbe

[8]There was a man living in Lystra whose feet were
crippled; he had been lame from birth and had never
been able to walk. [9]Sitting there, he listened to Paul's
words. Paul saw that he believed and could be healed,
so he looked straight at him [10]and said in a loud voice,
"Stand up straight on your feet!" The man jumped up
and started walking around. [11]When the crowds saw
what Paul had done, they started to shout in their own
Lycaonian language, "The gods have become like men
and have come down to us!" [12]They gave Barnabas the
name Zeus, and Paul the name Hermes, because he was
the one who did the speaking. [13]The priest of the god
Zeus, whose temple stood just outside the town, brought
bulls and flowers to the gate. He and the crowds wanted
to offer sacrifice to the apostles.

[14]When Barnabas and Paul heard what they were
about to do, they tore their clothes and ran into the
middle of the crowd, shouting, [15]"Why are you doing
this, men? We are just men, human beings like you! We
are here to announce the Good News, to turn you away
from these worthless things to the living God, who made
heaven, earth, sea, and all that is in them. [16]In the past
he allowed all peoples to go their own way. [17]But he has
always given proof of himself by the good things he
does: he gives you rain from heaven and crops at the
right times; he gives you food and fills your hearts with

*And dragged him out of town*

happiness." 18Even with these words the apostles could hardly keep the crowds from offering a sacrifice to them.

19Some Jews came from Antioch of Pisidia and from Iconium; they won the crowds to their side, stoned Paul and dragged him out of town, thinking that he was dead. 20But when the believers gathered around him, he got up and went back into the town. The next day he and Barnabas went to Derbe.

## The Return to Antioch in Syria

21Paul and Barnabas preached the Good News in Derbe, and won many disciples. Then they went back to Lystra, then to Iconium, and then to Antioch of Pisidia. 22They strengthened the believers and encouraged them to remain true to the faith. "We must pass through many troubles to enter the Kingdom of God," they taught. 23In each church they appointed elders for them; and with prayers and fasting they commended them to the Lord, in whom they had put their trust.

24After going through the territory of Pisidia, they came to Pamphylia. 25They preached the message in Perga and then went down to Attalia, 26and from there they sailed back to Antioch, the place where they had been commended to the care of God's grace for the work they had now completed.

<sup>27</sup>When they arrived in Antioch they gathered the people of the church together and told them of all that God had done with them, and how he had opened the way for the Gentiles to believe. <sup>28</sup>They stayed a long time there with the believers.

## The Meeting at Jerusalem

15 Some men came from Judea to Antioch and started teaching the brothers, "You cannot be saved unless you are circumcised as the Law of Moses requires." <sup>2</sup>Paul and Barnabas had a fierce argument and dispute with them about this; so it was decided that Paul and Barnabas and some of the others in Antioch should go to Jerusalem and see the apostles and elders about this matter.

<sup>3</sup>They were sent on their way by the church, and as they went through Phoenicia and Samaria they reported how the Gentiles had turned to God; this news brought great joy to all the brothers. <sup>4</sup>When they arrived in Jerusalem, they were welcomed by the church, the apostles, and the elders, to whom they told all that God had done with them. <sup>5</sup>But some of the believers who belonged to the party of the Pharisees stood up and said, "They have to be circumcised and told to obey the Law of Moses."

<sup>6</sup>The apostles and the elders met together to consider this question. <sup>7</sup>After a long debate Peter stood up and said, "My brothers, you know that a long time ago God chose me from among you to preach the message of Good News to the Gentiles, so that they could hear and believe. <sup>8</sup>And God, who knows the hearts of men, showed his approval of the Gentiles by giving the Holy Spirit to them, just as he had to us. <sup>9</sup>He made no difference between us and them; he purified their hearts because they believed. <sup>10</sup>So then, why do you want to put God to the test now by laying a load on the backs of the believers which neither our ancestors nor we ourselves were able to carry? <sup>11</sup>No! We believe and are saved by the grace of the Lord Jesus, just as they are."

<sup>12</sup>The whole group was silent as they heard Barnabas and Paul report all the wonders and miracles that God had done through them among the Gentiles. <sup>13</sup>When

they finished speaking, James spoke up, "Listen to me, brothers! [14]Simon has just explained how God first showed his care for the Gentiles by taking from among them a people to be all his own. [15]The words of the prophets agree completely with this. As the scripture says,

[16] 'After this I will return, says the Lord,
     and I will raise David's fallen house.
  I will restore its ruins,
     and build it up again.
[17] And so all other people will seek the Lord,
     all the Gentiles whom I have called to
     be my own.
[18] So says the Lord, who made this known
     long ago.'

[19]"It is my opinion," James went on, "that we should not trouble the Gentiles who are turning to God. [20]Instead, we should write a letter telling them not to eat any food that is unclean because it has been offered to idols; to keep themselves from immorality; not to eat any animal that has been strangled, or any blood. [21]For the Law of Moses has been read for a very long time in the synagogues every Sabbath, and his words are preached in every town."

## The Letter to the Gentile Believers

[22]Then the apostles and the elders, together with the whole church, decided to choose some men from the group and send them to Antioch with Paul and Barnabas. They chose Judas, called Barsabbas, and Silas, two men who were highly respected by the brothers. [23]They sent the following letter by them:

"We, the apostles and the elders, your brothers, send greetings to all brothers of Gentile birth who live in Antioch, Syria, and Cilicia. [24]We have heard that some men of our group went out and troubled and upset you by what they said; they had not, however, received any instructions from us to do this. [25]And so we have met together and have all agreed to choose some messengers and send them to you. They will go with our dear friends Barnabas and Paul, [26]who have risked their lives in the service of our Lord Jesus Christ. [27]We send you, then,

Judas and Silas, who will tell you in person the same things we are writing. [28]The Holy Spirit and we have agreed not to put any other burden on you besides these necessary rules: [29]eat no food that has been offered to idols; eat no blood; eat no animal that has been strangled; and keep yourselves from immorality. You will do well if you keep yourselves from doing these things. Good-bye."

[30]The messengers were sent off and went to Antioch, where they gathered the whole group of believers and gave them the letter. [31]When the people read the letter, they were filled with joy by the message of encouragement. [32]Judas and Silas, who were themselves prophets, spoke a long time with the brothers, giving them courage and strength. [33]After spending some time there, they were sent off in peace by the brothers, and went back to those who had sent them. [[34]But Silas decided to stay there.]

[35]Paul and Barnabas spent some time in Antioch. Together with many others, they taught and preached the word of the Lord.

## Paul and Barnabas Separate

[36]Some time later Paul said to Barnabas, "Let us go back and visit our brothers in every city where we preached the word of the Lord, and find out how they are getting along." [37]Barnabas wanted to take John Mark with them, [38]but Paul did not think it was right to take him, because he had not stayed with them to the end of their mission, but had turned back and left them in Pamphylia. [39]They had a sharp argument between them, and separated from each other. Barnabas took Mark and sailed off for Cyprus, [40]while Paul chose Silas and left, commended by the brothers to the care of the Lord's grace. [41]He went through Syria and Cilicia, strengthening the churches.

## Timothy Goes with Paul and Silas

16    Paul traveled on to Derbe and Lystra. A believer named Timothy lived there; his mother, also a

believer, was Jewish, but his father was Greek. ²All the brothers in Lystra and Iconium spoke well of Timothy. ³Paul wanted to take Timothy along with him, so he circumcised him. He did so because all the Jews who lived in those places knew that Timothy's father was Greek. ⁴As they went through the towns they delivered to the believers the rules decided upon by the apostles and elders in Jerusalem, and told them to obey these rules. ⁵So the churches were made stronger in the faith and grew in numbers every day.

## In Troas: Paul's Vision

⁶They traveled through the region of Phrygia and Galatia, because the Holy Spirit did not let them preach the message in the province of Asia. ⁷When they reached the border of Mysia, they tried to go into the province of Bithynia, but the Spirit of Jesus did not allow them. ⁸So they traveled right on through Mysia and went down to Troas. ⁹Paul had a vision that night in which he saw a man of Macedonia standing and begging him, "Come over to Macedonia and help us!" ¹⁰As soon as Paul had this vision, we got ready to leave for Macedonia, because we decided that God had called us to preach the Good News to the people there.

## In Philippi: the Conversion of Lydia

¹¹We left by ship from Troas and sailed straight across to Samothrace, and the next day to Neapolis. ¹²From there we went inland to Philippi, a city of the first district of Macedonia; it is also a Roman colony. We spent several days in that city. ¹³On the Sabbath day we went out of the city to the riverside, where we thought there would be a Jewish place for prayer. We sat down and talked to the women who gathered there. ¹⁴One of those who heard us was Lydia, from Thyatira, who was a dealer in purple goods. She was a woman who worshiped God, and the Lord opened her mind to pay attention to what Paul was saying. ¹⁵She and the people of her house were baptized. Then she invited us, "Come and stay in my house, if you have decided that I am a true believer in the Lord." And she persuaded us to go.

## In Prison at Philippi

<sup>16</sup>One day as we were going to the place of prayer, we were met by a slave girl who had an evil spirit in her that made her predict the future. She earned much money for her owners by telling fortunes. <sup>17</sup>She followed Paul and us, shouting, "These men are servants of the Most High God! They announce to you how you can be saved!" <sup>18</sup>She did this for many days, until Paul became so upset that he turned around and said to the spirit, "In the name of Jesus Christ I order you to come out of her!" The spirit went out of her that very moment. <sup>19</sup>When her owners realized that their chance of making money was gone, they grabbed Paul and Silas and dragged them to the authorities in the public square. <sup>20</sup>They brought them before the Roman officials and said, "These men are Jews, and they are causing trouble in our city. <sup>21</sup>They are teaching customs that are against our law; we are Romans and cannot accept or practice them." <sup>22</sup>The crowd joined the attack against them; the officials tore the clothes off Paul and Silas, and ordered them to be whipped. <sup>23</sup>After a severe beating they were thrown into jail, and the jailer was ordered to lock them up tight. <sup>24</sup>Upon receiving this order, the jailer threw them into the inner cell and fastened their feet between heavy blocks of wood.

<sup>25</sup>About midnight Paul and Silas were praying and singing hymns to God, and the other prisoners were listening to them. <sup>26</sup>Suddenly there was a violent earthquake, which shook the prison to its foundations. At once all the doors opened, and the chains fell off all the prisoners. <sup>27</sup>The jailer woke up, and when he saw the prison doors open he thought that all the prisoners had escaped; so he pulled out his sword and was about to kill himself. <sup>28</sup>But Paul shouted at the top of his voice, "Don't harm yourself! We are all here!"

<sup>29</sup>The jailer called for a light, rushed in, and fell trembling at the feet of Paul and Silas. <sup>30</sup>Then he led them out and asked, "What must I do, sirs, to be saved?"

<sup>31</sup>"Believe in the Lord Jesus," they said, "and you will be saved—you and your family." <sup>32</sup>Then they preached the word of the Lord to him and to all the

*What must I do, sirs, to be saved?*

others in his house. ³³At that very hour of the night the jailer took them and washed off their wounds; and he and all his family were baptized at once. ³⁴He took Paul and Silas up into his house and gave them some food to eat. He and his family were filled with joy, because he now believed in God.

³⁵The next morning the Roman authorities sent police officers with the order, "Let those men go."

³⁶So the jailer told it to Paul, "The officials have sent an order for you and Silas to be released. You may leave, then, and go in peace."

³⁷But Paul said to the police officers, "We were not found guilty of any crime, yet they whipped us in public—and we are Roman citizens! Then they threw us in prison. And now they want to send us away secretly? Not at all! The Roman officials themselves must come here and let us out."

³⁸The police officers reported these words to the Roman officials; and when they heard that Paul and Silas were Roman citizens, they were afraid. ³⁹So they went and apologized to them; then they led them out of the

prison and asked them to leave the city. [40]Paul and
Silas left the prison and went to Lydia's house. There
they met the brothers, spoke words of encouragement
to them, and left.

### In Thessalonica

**17** They traveled on through Amphipolis and Apol-
lonia, and came to Thessalonica, where there was
a Jewish synagogue. [2]According to his usual habit, Paul
went to the synagogue. There during three Sabbath days
he argued with the people from the Scriptures, [3]explain-
ing them and proving from them that the Messiah had
to suffer, and rise from death. "This Jesus whom I announce to you," Paul said, "is the Messiah." [4]Some of
them were convinced and joined Paul and Silas; so did
a large group of Greeks who worshiped God, and many
of the leading women.

[5]But the Jews were jealous and gathered some of the
worthless loafers from the streets and formed a mob.
They set the whole city in an uproar, and attacked the
home of Jason, trying to find Paul and Silas and bring
them out to the people. [6]But when they did not find
them, they dragged Jason and some other brothers to
the city authorities and shouted, "These men have
caused trouble everywhere! Now they have come to our
city, [7]and Jason has kept them in his house. They are all
breaking the laws of the Emperor, saying that there is
another king, by the name of Jesus." [8]With these words
they threw the crowd and the city authorities in an
uproar. [9]The authorities made Jason and the others pay
the required amount of money to be released, and then
let them go.

### In Berea

[10]As soon as night came, the brothers sent Paul and
Silas to Berea. When they arrived, they went to the
Jewish synagogue. [11]The people there were more open-
minded than the people in Thessalonica. They listened
to the message with great eagerness, and every day they
studied the Scriptures to see if what Paul said was really
true. [12]Many of them believed; and many Greek women
of high social standing and many Greek men also be-

lieved. [13]But when the Jews in Thessalonica heard that Paul had preached the word of God in Berea also, they came there and started exciting and stirring up the mobs. [14]At once the brothers sent Paul away to the coast; but both Silas and Timothy stayed in Berea. [15]The men who were taking Paul went with him as far as Athens. Then they went back to Berea with instructions from Paul that Silas and Timothy join him as soon as possible.

## In Athens

[16]While Paul was waiting in Athens for Silas and Timothy, he was greatly upset when he noticed how full of idols the city was. [17]So he argued in the synagogue with the Jews and the Gentiles who worshiped God, and in the public square every day with the people who happened to come by. [18]Certain Epicurean and Stoic teachers also debated with him. Some said, "What is this ignorant show-off trying to say?"

Others said, "He seems to be talking about foreign gods." They said this because Paul was preaching about Jesus and the resurrection. [19]So they took Paul, brought him before the meeting of the Areopagus, and said, "We would like to know this new teaching that you are talking about. [20]Some of the things we hear you say sound strange to us, and we would like to know what they mean." [21](For all the citizens of Athens and the foreigners who lived there liked to spend all their time telling and hearing the latest new thing.)

[22]Paul stood up in front of the meeting of the Areopagus and said, "Men of Athens! I see that in every way you are very religious. [23]For as I walked through your city and looked at the places where you worship, I found also an altar on which is written, 'To an Unknown God.' That which you worship, then, even though you do not know it, is what I now proclaim to you. [24]God, who made the world and everything in it, is Lord of heaven and earth, and does not live in temples made by men. [25]Nor does he need anything that men can supply by working for him, since it is he himself who gives life and breath and everything else to all men. [26]From the one man he created all races of men, and made them live

over the whole earth. He himself fixed beforehand the
exact times and the limits of the places where they
would live. [27]He did this so that they would look for
him, and perhaps find him as they felt around for him.
Yet God is actually not far from any one of us; [28]as
someone has said,

      'In him we live and move and exist.'
It is as some of your poets have said,

      'We too are his children.'
[29]Since we are God's children, we should not suppose
that his nature is anything like an image of gold or silver
or stone, shaped by the art and skill of man. [30]God has
overlooked the times when men did not know, but now
he commands all men everywhere to turn away from
their evil ways. [31]For he has fixed a day in which he will
judge the whole world with justice, by means of a man
he has chosen. He has given proof of this to everyone
by raising that man from death!"

[32]When they heard Paul speak about a raising from
death, some of them made fun of him, but others said,
"We want to hear you speak about this again." [33]And
so Paul left the meeting. [34]Some men joined him and
believed; among them was Dionysius, a member of the
Areopagus, a woman named Damaris, and some
others.

### In Corinth

18 After this, Paul left Athens and went on to Corinth. [2]There he met a Jew named Aquila, born in
Pontus, who had just come from Italy with his wife
Priscilla, because Emperor Claudius had ordered all the
Jews to leave Rome. Paul went to see them, [3]and stayed
and worked with them, because he earned his living by
making tents, just as they did. [4]He argued in the synagogue every Sabbath, trying to convince both Jews and
Greeks.

[5]When Silas and Timothy arrived from Macedonia,
Paul gave his whole time to preaching the message,
testifying to the Jews that Jesus is the Messiah. [6]When
they opposed him and said evil things about him, he
protested by shaking the dust from his clothes and saying to them, "If you are lost, you yourselves must take
the blame for it! I am not responsible. From now on I

*He earned his living by making tents*

will go to the Gentiles." <sup>7</sup>So he left them and went to live in the house of a Gentile named Titius Justus, who worshiped God; his house was next to the synagogue. <sup>8</sup>Crispus, the leader of the synagogue, believed in the Lord, he and all his family; and many other people in Corinth heard the message, believed, and were baptized.

<sup>9</sup>One night Paul had a vision, in which the Lord said to him, "Do not be afraid, but keep on speaking and do not give up, <sup>10</sup>because I am with you. No one will be able to harm you, because many in this city are my people." <sup>11</sup>So Paul stayed there for a year and a half, teaching the people the word of God.

<sup>12</sup>When Gallio was made the Roman governor of Greece, the Jews got together, seized Paul and took him into court. <sup>13</sup>"This man," they said, "is trying to persuade people to worship God in a way that is against the law!"

<sup>14</sup>Paul was about to speak, when Gallio said to the Jews, "If this were a matter of some wrong or evil crime that has been committed, it would be reasonable for me to be patient with you Jews. <sup>15</sup>But since it is an argument about words and names and your own law, you yourselves must settle it. I will not be the judge of such things!" <sup>16</sup>And he drove them out of the court.

[17]They all grabbed Sosthenes, the leader of the synagogue, and beat him in front of the court. But that did not bother Gallio a bit.

## The Return to Antioch

[18]Paul stayed on in Corinth with the brothers for many days, then left them and sailed off with Priscilla and Aquila for Syria. Before sailing he made a vow in Cenchreae and had his head shaved. [19]They arrived in Ephesus, where Paul left Priscilla and Aquila. He went into the synagogue and argued with the Jews. [20]They asked him to stay with them a long time, but he would not consent. [21]Instead, he told them as he left, "If it is the will of God, I will come back to you." And so he sailed from Ephesus.

[22]When he arrived at Caesarea he went to Jerusalem and greeted the church, and then went to Antioch. [23]After spending some time there he left. He went through the region of Galatia and Phrygia, strengthening all the believers.

## Apollos in Ephesus and Corinth

[24]A certain Jew named Apollos, born in Alexandria, came to Ephesus. He was an eloquent speaker and had a thorough knowledge of the Scriptures. [25]He had been instructed in the Way of the Lord, and with great enthusiasm spoke and taught correctly the facts about Jesus. However, he knew only the baptism of John. [26]He began to speak boldly in the synagogue. When Priscilla and Aquila heard him, they took him home with them and explained to him more correctly the Way of God. [27]Apollos decided to go to Greece, so the believers in Ephesus helped him by writing to their brothers in Greece, urging them to welcome him there. When he arrived, he was a great help to those who through God's grace had become believers. [28]For with his strong arguments he defeated the Jews in public debates, proving from the Scriptures that Jesus is the Messiah.

## Paul in Ephesus

**19** While Apollos was in Corinth, Paul traveled through the interior of the province and arrived in Ephesus. There he found some disciples, ²and asked them, "Did you receive the Holy Spirit when you believed?"

"We have not even heard that there is a Holy Spirit," they answered.

³"Well, then, what kind of baptism did you receive?" Paul asked.

"The baptism of John," they answered.

⁴Paul said, "The baptism of John was for those who turned from their sins; and he told the people of Israel to believe in the one who was coming after him—that is, in Jesus."

⁵When they heard this, they were baptized in the name of the Lord Jesus. ⁶Paul placed his hands on them, and the Holy Spirit came upon them; they spoke in strange tongues and also proclaimed God's message. ⁷They were about twelve men in all.

⁸Paul went into the synagogue, and for three months spoke boldly with the people, arguing with them and trying to convince them about the Kingdom of God. ⁹But some of them were stubborn and would not believe, and said evil things about the Way of the Lord before the whole group. So Paul left them and took the disciples with him; and every day he held discussions in the lecture hall of Tyrannus. ¹⁰This went on for two years, so that all the people who lived in the province of Asia, both Jews and Gentiles, heard the word of the Lord.

## The Sons of Sceva

¹¹God was performing unusual miracles through Paul. ¹²Even handkerchiefs and aprons he had used were taken to the sick, and their diseases were driven away and the evil spirits would go out of them. ¹³Some Jews who traveled around and drove out evil spirits also tried to use the name of the Lord Jesus to do this. They said to the evil spirits, "I command you in the name of Jesus, whom Paul preaches." ¹⁴There were seven sons of a Jewish High Priest named Sceva who were doing this.

¹⁵But the evil spirit said to them, "I know Jesus and I know about Paul; but you—who are you?"

¹⁶The man who had the evil spirit in him attacked them with such violence that he defeated them. They all

ran away from his house, wounded and with their clothes torn off. [17]All the Jews and Gentiles who lived in Ephesus heard about this; they were all filled with fear, and the name of the Lord Jesus was given greater honor. [18]Many of the believers came, publicly admitting and revealing what they had done. [19]Many of those who had practiced magic brought their books together and burned them in the presence of everyone. They added up the price of the books and the total came to fifty thousand dollars. [20]In this powerful way the word of the Lord kept spreading and growing stronger.

## The Riot in Ephesus

[21]After these things had happened, Paul made up his mind to travel through Macedonia and Greece and go on to Jerusalem. "After I go there," he said, "I must also see Rome." [22]So he sent Timothy and Erastus, two of his helpers, to Macedonia, while he spent more time in the province of Asia.

[23]It was at this time that there was serious trouble in Ephesus because of the Way of the Lord. [24]A certain silversmith named Demetrius made silver models of the temple of the goddess Artemis, and his business brought a great deal of profit to the workers. [25]So he called them all together, with others whose work was like theirs, and said to them, "Men, you know that our prosperity comes from this work. [26]You can see and hear for yourselves what this fellow Paul is doing. He says that gods made by men are not gods at all, and has succeeded in convincing many people, both here in Ephesus and in nearly the whole province of Asia. [27]There is the danger, then, that this business of ours will get a bad name. Not only that, there is also the danger that the temple of the great goddess Artemis will come to mean nothing, and that her greatness will be destroyed—the goddess worshiped by everyone in Asia and in all the world!"

[28]As the crowd heard these words they became furious, and started shouting, "Great is Artemis of Ephesus!" [29]The uproar spread throughout the whole city. The mob grabbed Gaius and Aristarchus, two Macedonians who were traveling with Paul, and rushed with them to the theater. [30]Paul himself wanted to go before the crowd, but the believers would not let him.

³¹Some of the provincial authorities, who were his friends, also sent him a message begging him not to show himself in the theater. ³²Meanwhile, the whole meeting was in an uproar: some people were shouting one thing, others were shouting something else, because most of them did not even know why they had come together. ³³Some of the people concluded that Alexander was responsible, since the Jews made him go up to the front. Then Alexander motioned with his hand and tried to make a speech of defense before the people. ³⁴But when they recognized that he was a Jew, they all shouted together the same thing for two hours, "Great is Artemis of Ephesus!"

³⁵At last the city clerk was able to calm the crowd. "Men of Ephesus!" he said. "Everyone knows that the city of Ephesus is the keeper of the temple of the great Artemis and of the sacred stone that fell down from heaven. ³⁶Nobody can deny these things. So then, you must calm down and not do anything reckless. ³⁷You have brought these men here, even though they have not robbed temples or said evil things about our goddess. ³⁸If Demetrius and his workers have an accusation against someone, there are the regular days for court and there are the authorities; they can accuse each other there. ³⁹But if there is something more that you want, it will have to be settled in the legal meeting of citizens. ⁴⁰For there is the danger that we will be accused of a riot in what has happened today. There is no excuse for all this uproar, and we would not be able to give a good reason for it." ⁴¹After saying this, he dismissed the meeting.

## To Macedonia and Greece

**20** After the uproar died down, Paul called together the believers, and with words of encouragement said good-bye to them. Then he left and went on to Macedonia. ²He went through those regions and encouraged the people with many messages. Then he came to Greece, ³where he stayed three months. He was getting ready to go to Syria when he discovered that the Jews were plotting against him; so he decided to go back through Macedonia. ⁴Sopater, the son of Pyrrhus, from

Berea, went with him; so did Aristarchus and Secundus, from Thessalonica; Gaius, from Derbe; Timothy; and Tychicus and Trophimus, from the province of Asia. [5]They went ahead and waited for us in Troas. [6]We sailed from Philippi after the Feast of Unleavened Bread, and five days later joined them in Troas, where we spent a week.

*Eutychus got sleepier and sleepier*

## Paul's Last Visit in Troas

[7]On Saturday evening we gathered together for the fellowship meal. Paul spoke to the people, and kept on speaking until midnight, since he was going to leave the next day. [8]There were many lamps in the upstairs room where we were meeting. [9]A young man named Eutychus was sitting in the window; and as Paul kept on talking, Eutychus got sleepier and sleepier, until he finally went sound asleep and fell from the third story to the ground. They picked him up, and he was dead.

[10]But Paul went down and threw himself on him and hugged him. "Don't worry," he said, "he is still alive!" [11]Then he went back upstairs, broke bread, and ate. After talking with them for a long time until sunrise, Paul left. [12]They took the young man home alive, and were greatly comforted.

## From Troas to Miletus

[13]We went on ahead to the ship and sailed off to Assos, where we were going to take Paul aboard. He had told us to do this, because he was going there by land. [14]When he met us in Assos, we took him aboard and went on to Mitylene. [15]We sailed from there and arrived off Chios the next day. A day later we came to Samos, and the following day we reached Miletus. [16]Paul had decided to sail on by Ephesus, so as not to lose any time in the province of Asia. He was in a hurry to arrive in Jerusalem, if at all possible, by the day of Pentecost.

## Paul's Farewell Speech to the Elders of Ephesus

[17]Paul sent a message from Miletus to Ephesus, asking the elders of the church to meet him. [18]When they arrived, he said to them, "You know how I spent the whole time I was with you, from the first day I arrived in the province of Asia. [19]With all humility and many tears I did my work as the Lord's servant, through the hard times that came to me because of the plots of the Jews. [20]You know that I did not hold back anything that would be of help to you as I preached and taught you in public and in your homes. [21]To Jews and Gentiles alike I gave solemn warning that they should turn from their sins to God, and believe in our Lord Jesus. [22]And now, in obedience to the Holy Spirit, I am going to Jerusalem, not knowing what will happen to me there. [23]I only know that in every city the Holy Spirit has warned me that prison and troubles wait for me. [24]But I reckon my own life to be worth nothing to me, in order that I may complete my mission and finish the work that the Lord Jesus gave me to do, which is to declare the Good News of the grace of God.

[25]"I have gone about among all of you, preaching the Kingdom of God. And now I know that none of you will

ever see me again. <sup>26</sup>So I solemnly declare to you this very day: if any of you should be lost, I am not responsible. <sup>27</sup>For I have not held back from announcing to you the whole purpose of God. <sup>28</sup>Keep watch over yourselves and over all the flock which the Holy Spirit has placed in your care. Be shepherds of the church of God, which he made his own through the death of his own Son. <sup>29</sup>I know that after I leave, fierce wolves will come among you, and they will not spare the flock. <sup>30</sup>The time will come when some men from your own group will tell lies to lead the believers away after them. <sup>31</sup>Watch, then, and remember that with many tears, day and night, I taught every one of you for three years.

<sup>32</sup>"And now I place you in the care of God and the message of his grace. He is able to build you up and give you the blessings he keeps for all his people. <sup>33</sup>I have not coveted anyone's silver or gold or clothing. <sup>34</sup>You yourselves know that with these hands of mine I have worked and provided everything that my companions and I have needed. <sup>35</sup>I have shown you in all things that by working hard in this way we must help the weak, remembering the words that the Lord Jesus himself said, 'There is more happiness in giving than in receiving.' "

<sup>36</sup>When Paul finished, he knelt down with them all and prayed. <sup>37</sup>They were all crying as they hugged him and kissed him good-bye. <sup>38</sup>They were especially sad at the words he had said that they would never see him again. And so they went with him to the ship.

## Paul Goes to Jerusalem

21   We said good-bye to them and left. After sailing straight across, we came to Cos; the next day we reached Rhodes, and from there we went on to Patara. <sup>2</sup>There we found a ship that was going to Phoenicia; so we went aboard and sailed away. <sup>3</sup>We came to where we could see Cyprus, and sailed south of it on to Syria. We went ashore at Tyre, where the ship was going to unload its cargo. <sup>4</sup>We found some believers there, and stayed with them a week. By the power of the Spirit they told Paul not to go to Jerusalem. <sup>5</sup>But when our time with them was over, we left and went on our way. All of

*Knelt down on the beach and prayed*

them, with their wives and children, went with us out of the city. We all knelt down on the beach and prayed. ⁶Then we said good-bye to one another, and we went on board the ship while they went back home.

⁷We continued our voyage, sailing from Tyre to Ptolemais, where we greeted the brothers and stayed with them for a day. ⁸On the following day we left and arrived in Caesarea. There we went to the house of the evangelist Philip, and stayed with him. He was one of the seven men who had been chosen in Jerusalem. ⁹He had four unmarried daughters who proclaimed God's message. ¹⁰We had been there for several days when a prophet named Agabus arrived from Judea. ¹¹He came to us, took Paul's belt, tied up his own feet and hands with it, and said, "This is what the Holy Spirit says: The owner of this belt will be tied up in this way by the Jews in Jerusalem, and they will hand him over to the Gentiles."

¹²When we heard this, we and the others there begged Paul not to go to Jerusalem. ¹³But he answered, "What are you doing, crying like this and breaking my heart? I am ready not only to be tied up in Jerusalem but even to die there for the sake of the Lord Jesus."

¹⁴We could not convince him, so we gave up and said, "May the Lord's will be done."

¹⁵After spending some time there, we got our things ready and left for Jerusalem. ¹⁶Some of the disciples from Caesarea also went with us, and took us to the house of the man we were going to stay with—Mna-

son, from Cyprus, who had been a believer since the early days.

## Paul Visits James

[17]When we arrived in Jerusalem the brothers welcomed us warmly. [18]The next day Paul went with us to see James; and all the church elders were present. [19]Paul greeted them and gave a complete report of everything that God had done among the Gentiles through his work. [20]After hearing him, they all praised God. Then they said to Paul, "You can see how it is, brother. There are thousands of Jews who have become believers, and they are all very devoted to the Law. [21]They have been told about you that you have been teaching all the Jews who live in Gentile countries to abandon the Law of Moses, telling them not to circumcise their children or follow the Jewish customs. [22]They are sure to hear that you have arrived. What should be done, then? [23]Do what we tell you. There are four men here who have taken a vow. [24]Go along with them and join them in the ceremony of purification and pay their expenses; then they will be able to shave their heads. In this way everyone will know that there is no truth in any of the things that they have been told about you, but that you yourself live in accordance with the Law of Moses. [25]But as to the Gentiles who have become believers, we have sent them a letter telling them we decided that they must not eat any food that has been offered to idols, or any blood, or any animal that has been strangled, and that they must keep themselves from immorality."

[26]So Paul took the men and the next day performed the ceremony of purification with them. Then he went into the temple and gave notice of how many days it would be until the end of the period of purification, when the sacrifice for each one of them would be offered.

## Paul Arrested in the Temple

[27]When the seven days were about to come to an end, some Jews from the province of Asia saw Paul in the temple. They stirred up the whole crowd and grabbed

Paul. [28]"Men of Israel!" they shouted. "Help! This is the man who goes everywhere teaching everyone against the people of Israel, the Law of Moses, and this temple. And now he has even brought some Gentiles into the temple and defiled this holy place!" [29](They said this because they had seen Trophimus from Ephesus with Paul in the city, and they thought that Paul had taken him into the temple.)

*The mob was trying to kill Paul*

[30]Confusion spread through the whole city, and the people all ran together, grabbed Paul, and dragged him out of the temple. At once the temple doors were closed. [31]The mob was trying to kill Paul when a report was sent up to the commander of the Roman troops that all of Jerusalem was rioting. [32]At once the commander took some officers and soldiers and rushed down to the crowd. When the people saw him with the soldiers, they stopped beating Paul. [33]The commander went over to Paul, arrested him, and ordered him to be tied up with two chains. Then he asked, "Who is this man, and what has he done?" [34]Some in the crowd shouted one thing, others something else. There was such confusion that the commander could not find out exactly what had happened; so he ordered his men to take Paul up into the fort. [35]They got with him to the steps, and then the soldiers had to carry him because the mob was so wild. [36]They were all coming after him and screaming, "Kill him!"

## Paul Defends Himself

<sup>37</sup>As they were about to take Paul into the fort, he
spoke to the commander, "May I say something to
you?"

"Do you speak Greek?" the commander asked.
<sup>38</sup>"Then you are not that Egyptian fellow who some
time ago started a revolution and led four thousand
armed terrorists out into the desert?"

<sup>39</sup>Paul answered, "I am a Jew, born in Tarsus of
Cilicia, a citizen of an important city. Please, let me
speak to the people."

<sup>40</sup>The commander gave him permission, so Paul
stood on the steps and motioned with his hand to the
people. When they were quiet, Paul spoke to them in
Hebrew,

22 "Men, brothers and fathers, listen to me as I
make my defense before you!" <sup>2</sup>When they heard
him speaking to them in Hebrew, they were even qui-
eter; and Paul went on,

<sup>3</sup>"I am a Jew, born in Tarsus of Cilicia, but brought up
here in Jerusalem as a student of Gamaliel. I received
strict instruction in the Law of our ancestors, and was
just as dedicated to God as all of you here today are. <sup>4</sup>I
persecuted to the death the people who followed this
Way. I arrested men and women and threw them into
prison. <sup>5</sup>The High Priest and the whole Council can
prove that I am telling the truth. I received from them
letters written to the Jewish brothers in Damascus, so I
went there to arrest these people and bring them back
in chains to Jerusalem to be punished."

## Paul Tells of His Conversion
(Also Acts 9.1–19; 26.12–18)

<sup>6</sup>"As I was traveling and coming near Damascus,
about midday a bright light from the sky flashed suddenly around me. <sup>7</sup>I fell to the ground and heard a voice
saying to me, 'Saul, Saul! Why do you persecute me?'
<sup>8</sup>'Who are you, Lord?' I asked. 'I am Jesus of Nazareth,
whom you persecute,' he said to me. <sup>9</sup>The men with me
saw the light but did not hear the voice of the one who
was speaking to me. <sup>10</sup>I asked, 'What shall I do, Lord?'
and the Lord said to me, 'Get up and go into Damascus,

and there you will be told everything that God has determined for you to do.' ¹¹I was blind because of the bright light, and so my companions took me by the hand and led me into Damascus.

¹²"There was a man named Ananias, a religious man who obeyed our Law and was highly respected by all the Jews living in Damascus. ¹³He came to me, stood by me and said, 'Brother Saul, see again!' At that very moment I saw again and looked at him. ¹⁴He said, 'The God of our ancestors has chosen you to know his will, to see his righteous Servant, and hear him speaking with his own voice. ¹⁵For you will be a witness for him to tell all men what you have seen and heard. ¹⁶And now, why wait any longer? Get up and be baptized and have your sins washed away by calling on his name.' "

## Paul's Call to Preach to the Gentiles

¹⁷"I went back to Jerusalem, and while I was praying in the temple I had a vision, ¹⁸in which I saw the Lord as he said to me, 'Hurry and leave Jerusalem quickly, because the people here will not accept your witness about me.' ¹⁹'Lord,' I answered, 'they know very well that I went to the synagogues and arrested and beat those who believe in you. ²⁰And when your witness Stephen was put to death, I myself was there, approving of his murder and taking care of the cloaks of his murderers.' ²¹'Go,' the Lord said to me, 'because I will send you far away to the Gentiles.' "

²²The people listened to Paul until he said this; but then they started shouting at the top of their voices, "Away with him! Kill him! He's not fit to live!" ²³They were screaming, waving their clothes, and throwing dust up in the air. ²⁴The Roman commander ordered his men to take Paul into the fort, and told them to whip him to find out why the Jews were screaming like this against him. ²⁵But when they had tied him up to be whipped, Paul said to the officer standing there, "Is it lawful for you to whip a Roman citizen who hasn't even been tried for any crime?"

²⁶When the officer heard this, he went to the commander and asked him, "What are you doing? That man is a Roman citizen!"

²⁷So the commander went to Paul and asked him, "Tell me, are you a Roman citizen?"

"Yes," answered Paul.

²⁸The commander said, "I became one by paying a large amount of money."

"But I am one by birth," Paul answered.

²⁹At once the men who were going to question Paul drew back from him; and the commander was afraid when he realized that Paul was a Roman citizen, and that he had put him in chains.

## Paul before the Council

³⁰The commander wanted to find out for sure what the Jews were accusing Paul of; so the next day he had Paul's chains taken off and ordered the chief priests and the whole Council to meet. Then he took Paul, and made him stand before them.

23 Paul looked straight at the Council and said, "My brothers! My conscience is perfectly clear about my whole life before God, to this very day." ²The High Priest Ananias ordered those who were standing close to Paul to strike him on the mouth. ³Paul said to him, "God will certainly strike you—you whitewashed wall! You sit there to judge me according to the Law, yet you break the Law by ordering them to strike me!"

⁴The men close to Paul said to him, "You are insulting God's High Priest!"

⁵Paul answered, "I did not know, my brothers, that he was the High Priest. The scripture says, 'You must not speak evil of the ruler of your people.'"

⁶When Paul saw that some of the group were Sadducees and that others were Pharisees, he called out in the Council, "My brothers! I am a Pharisee, the son of Pharisees. I am on trial here because I hope that the dead will rise to life!"

⁷As soon as he said this, the Pharisees and Sadducees started to quarrel, and the group was divided. ⁸(For the Sadducees say that people will not rise from death, and that there are no angels or spirits; but the Pharisees believe in all three.) ⁹The shouting became louder, and some of the teachers of the Law who belonged to the party of the Pharisees stood up and protested strongly, "We cannot

find a thing wrong with this man! Perhaps a spirit or an angel really did speak to him!"

[10]The argument became so violent that the commander was afraid that Paul would be torn to pieces by them. So he ordered his soldiers to go down into the group and get Paul away from them, and take him into the fort.

[11]The following night the Lord stood by Paul and said, "Courage! You have given your witness to me here in Jerusalem, and you must do the same in Rome also."

## The Plot against Paul's Life

[12]The next morning some Jews met together and made a plan. They took a vow that they would not eat or drink anything until they had killed Paul. [13]There were more than forty of them who planned this together. [14]Then they went to the chief priests and elders and said, "We have taken a solemn vow together not to eat a thing until we kill Paul. [15]Now then, you and the Council send word to the Roman commander to bring Paul down to you, pretending that you want to get more accurate information about him. But we will be ready to kill him before he ever gets here."

[16]But the son of Paul's sister heard of the plot; so he went and entered the fort and told it to Paul. [17]Then Paul called one of the officers and said to him, "Take this young man to the commander; he has something to tell him." [18]The officer took him, led him to the commander and said, "The prisoner Paul called me and asked me to bring this young man to you, because he has something to say to you."

[19]The commander took him by the hand, led him off by himself, and asked him, "What do you have to tell me?"

[20]He said, "The Jewish authorities have agreed to ask you tomorrow to take Paul down to the Council, pretending that the Council wants to get more accurate information about him. [21]But don't listen to them, because there are more than forty men who will be hiding and waiting for him. They have taken a vow not to eat or drink until they kill him. They are now ready to do it, and are waiting for your decision."

²²The commander said, "Don't tell anyone that you have reported this to me." And he sent the young man away.

## Paul Sent to Governor Felix

²³Then the commander called two of his officers and said, "Get two hundred soldiers ready to go to Caesarea, together with seventy horsemen and two hundred spearmen, and be ready to leave by nine o'clock tonight. ²⁴Provide some horses for Paul to ride, and get him safely through to Governor Felix." ²⁵Then the commander wrote a letter that went like this:

²⁶"Claudius Lysias to his Excellency, the Governor Felix: Greetings. ²⁷The Jews seized this man and were about to kill him. I learned that he is a Roman citizen, so I went with my soldiers and rescued him. ²⁸I wanted to know what they were accusing him of, so I took him down to their Council. ²⁹I found out that he had not done a thing for which he deserved to die or be put in prison; the accusation against him had to do with questions about their own law. ³⁰And when I was informed that some Jews were making a plot against him, I decided to send him to you. I told his accusers to make their charges against him before you."

³¹The soldiers carried out their orders. They got Paul and took him that night as far as Antipatris. ³²The next day the foot soldiers returned to the fort and left the horsemen to go on with him. ³³They took him to Caesarea, delivered the letter to the Governor, and turned Paul over to him. ³⁴The Governor read the letter and asked Paul what province he was from. When he found out that he was from Cilicia, ³⁵he said, "I will hear you when your accusers arrive." Then he gave orders that Paul be kept under guard in Herod's palace.

## Paul Accused by the Jews

24 Five days later the High Priest Ananias went to Caesarea with some elders and a lawyer named Tertullus. They appeared before Governor Felix and made their charges against Paul. ²Tertullus was called and began to accuse Paul as follows:

"Your Excellency! Your wise leadership has brought

us a long period of peace, and many necessary reforms are being made for the good of our country. ³We welcome this everywhere at all times, and we are deeply grateful to you. ⁴I do not want to take up too much of your time, however, so I beg you to be kind and listen to our brief account. ⁵We found this man to be a dangerous nuisance; he starts riots among the Jews all over the world, and is a leader of the party of the Nazarenes. ⁶He also tried to defile the temple, and we arrested him. [We planned to judge him according to our own Law, ⁷but the commander Lysias came in and with great violence took him from us. ⁸Then Lysias gave orders that his accusers should come before you.] If you question this man, you yourself will be able to learn from him all the things that we are accusing him of." ⁹The Jews joined in the accusation and said that all this was true.

## Paul's Defense before Felix

¹⁰The Governor then motioned to Paul to speak, and Paul said,

"I know that you have been a judge over this nation for many years, and so I am happy to defend myself before you. ¹¹As you can find out for yourself, it was no more than twelve days ago that I went up to Jerusalem to worship. ¹²The Jews did not find me arguing with anyone in the temple, nor did they find me stirring up the people, either in the synagogues or anywhere else in the city. ¹³Nor can they give you proof of the accusations they now bring against me. ¹⁴I do admit this to you: I worship the God of our ancestors by following that Way which they say is false. But I also believe in all the things written in the Law of Moses and the books of the prophets. ¹⁵I have the same hope in God that these themselves hold, that all men, both the good and the bad, will rise from death. ¹⁶And so I do my best always to have a clear conscience before God and men.

¹⁷"After being away from Jerusalem for several years, I went there to take some money to my own people and to offer sacrifices. ¹⁸It was while I was doing this that they found me in the temple, after I had completed the ceremony of purification. There was no crowd with me, and no disorder. ¹⁹But some Jews from the province of

Asia were there; they themselves ought to come before you and make their accusations, if they have anything against me. [20]Or let these men here tell what crime they found me guilty of when I stood before the Council— [21]except for the one thing I called out when I stood before them: 'I am being judged by you today for believing that the dead will rise to life.'"

[22]Then Felix, who was well informed about the Way, brought the hearing to a close. "I will decide your case," he told them, "when the commander Lysias arrives." [23]He ordered the officer in charge of Paul to keep him under guard, but to give him some freedom and allow his friends to provide for his needs.

## Paul before Felix and Drusilla

[24]After some days Felix came with his wife Drusilla, who was Jewish. He sent for Paul and listened to him as he talked about faith in Christ Jesus. [25]But as Paul went on discussing about goodness, self-control, and the coming Day of Judgment, Felix was afraid and said, "You may leave now. I will call you again when I get the chance." [26]At the same time he was hoping that Paul would give him some money; and for this reason he would call for him often and talk with him.

[27]After two years had passed, Porcius Festus took the place of Felix as Governor. Felix wanted to gain favor with the Jews, so he left Paul in prison.

## Paul Appeals to the Emperor

25 Three days after Festus arrived in the province, he went from Caesarea to Jerusalem. [2]There the chief priests and the Jewish leaders brought their charges against Paul. They begged Festus [3]to do them the favor of having Paul come to Jerusalem, because they had made a plot to kill him on the way. [4]Festus answered, "Paul is being kept a prisoner in Caesarea, and I myself will be going back there soon. [5]Let your leaders go to Caesarea with me and accuse the man, if he has done anything wrong."

[6]Festus spent another eight or ten days with them, and then went to Caesarea. On the next day he sat down in the judgment court, and ordered Paul to be brought

in. ⁷When Paul arrived, the Jews who had come from Jerusalem stood around him and started making many serious charges against him, which they were not able to prove. ⁸But Paul defended himself, "I have done nothing wrong against the Law of the Jews, or the temple, or the Roman Emperor."

⁹Festus wanted to gain favor with the Jews, so he asked Paul, "Would you be willing to go to Jerusalem and be tried on these charges before me there?"

¹⁰Paul said, "I am standing before the Emperor's own judgment court, where I should be tried. I have done no wrong to the Jews, as you yourself well know. ¹¹If I have broken the law and done something for which I deserve the death penalty, I do not ask to escape it. But if there is no truth in the charges they bring against me, no one can hand me over to them. I appeal to the Emperor."

¹²Then Festus, after conferring with his advisers, answered, "You have appealed to the Emperor, so to the Emperor you will go."

## Paul before Agrippa and Bernice

¹³Some time later King Agrippa and Bernice came to Caesarea to pay a visit of welcome to Festus. ¹⁴After they had been there several days, Festus explained Paul's situation to the king, "There is a man here who was left a prisoner by Felix; ¹⁵and when I went to Jerusalem, the Jewish chief priests and elders brought charges against him and asked me to condemn him. ¹⁶But I told them that the Romans are not in the habit of handing over any man accused of a crime before he has met his accusers face to face, and has the chance of defending himself against the accusation. ¹⁷When they came here, then, I lost no time, but on the very next day I sat in the judgment court and ordered the man to be brought in. ¹⁸His opponents stood up, but they did not accuse him of any of the evil crimes that I thought they would. ¹⁹All they had were some arguments with him about their own religion and about a man named Jesus, who has died; but Paul claims that he is alive. ²⁰I was undecided about how I could get information on these matters, so I asked Paul if he would be willing to go to Jerusalem

and be tried there on these charges. ²¹But Paul appealed; he asked to be kept under guard and let the Emperor decide his case. So I gave orders for him to be kept under guard until I could send him to the Emperor."

²²Agrippa said to Festus, "I would like to hear this man myself."

"You will hear him tomorrow," Festus answered.

²³The next day Agrippa and Bernice came with great pomp and ceremony, and entered the audience hall with the military chiefs and the leading men of the city. Festus gave the order and Paul was brought in. ²⁴Festus said, "King Agrippa, and all who are here with us: You see this man against whom all the Jewish people, both here and in Jerusalem, have brought complaints to me. They scream that he should not live any longer. ²⁵But I could not find that he had done anything for which he deserved the death sentence. And since he himself made an appeal to the Emperor, I have decided to send him. ²⁶But I do not have anything definite about him to write to the Emperor. So I have brought him here before you—and especially before you, King Agrippa!—so that, after investigating his case, I may have something to write. ²⁷For it seems unreasonable to me to send a prisoner without clearly indicating the charges against him."

## Paul Defends Himself before Agrippa

26 Agrippa said to Paul, "You have permission to speak on your own behalf." Paul stretched out his hand and defended himself as follows:

²"King Agrippa! I consider myself fortunate that today I am to defend myself before you from all the things the Jews accuse me of. ³This is especially true because you know so well all the Jewish customs and questions. I ask you, then, to listen to me with patience.

⁴"All the Jews know how I have lived ever since I was young. They know from the beginning how I have spent my whole life in my own country and in Jerusalem. ⁵They have always known, if they are willing to testify, that from the very first I have lived as a member of the strictest party of our religion, the Pharisees. ⁶And now I stand here to be tried because I hope in the promise that God made to our ancestors—⁷the very promise that

all twelve tribes of our people hope to receive, as they worship God day and night. And it is because of this hope, your Majesty, that I am being accused by the Jews! ⁸Why do you Jews find it impossible to believe that God raises the dead?

⁹"I myself thought that I should do everything I could against the name of Jesus of Nazareth. ¹⁰That is what I did in Jerusalem. I received authority from the chief priests and put many of God's people in prison; and when they were sentenced to death, I also voted for it. ¹¹Many times I had them punished in all the synagogues, and tried to make them deny their faith. I was so furious with them that I even went to foreign cities to persecute them."

## Paul Tells of His Conversion
*(Also Acts 9.1–19; 22.6–16)*

¹²"It was for this purpose that I went to Damascus with the authority and orders from the chief priests. ¹³It was on the road at midday, your Majesty, that I saw a light much brighter than the sun shining from the sky around me and the men traveling with me. ¹⁴All of us fell to the ground, and I heard a voice say to me in the Hebrew language, 'Saul, Saul! Why are you persecuting me? You hurt yourself by hitting back, like an ox kicking against its owner's stick.' ¹⁵'Who are you, Lord?' I asked. And the Lord said: 'I am Jesus, whom you persecute. ¹⁶But get up and stand on your feet. I have appeared to you to appoint you as my servant; you are to tell others what you have seen of me today, and what I will show you in the future. ¹⁷I will save you from the people of Israel and from the Gentiles, to whom I will send you. ¹⁸You are to open their eyes and turn them from the darkness to the light, and from the power of Satan to God, so that through their faith in me they will have their sins forgiven and receive their place among God's chosen people.' "

## Paul Tells of His Work

¹⁹"And so, King Agrippa, I did not disobey the vision I had from heaven. ²⁰First in Damascus and in Jerusalem, and then in the whole country of the Jews and among the Gentiles, I preached that they must repent of

their sins and turn to God, and do the things that would show they had repented. [21]It was for this reason that the Jews seized me while I was in the temple, and tried to kill me. [22]But to this very day I have been helped by God, and so I stand here giving my witness to all, to the small and great alike. What I say is the very same thing the prophets and Moses said was going to happen: [23]that the Messiah must suffer and be the first one to rise from death, to announce the light of salvation to the Jews and to the Gentiles."

[24]As Paul defended himself in this way, Festus shouted at him, "You are mad, Paul! Your great learning is driving you mad!"

[25]Paul answered, "I am not mad, your Excellency! The words I speak are true and sober. [26]King Agrippa! I can speak to you with all boldness, because you know about these things. I am sure that you have taken notice of every one of them, for this thing has not happened hidden away in a corner. [27]King Agrippa, do you believe the prophets? I know that you do!"

[28]Agrippa said to Paul, "In this short time do you think you will make me a Christian?"

[29]"Whether a short time or a long time," Paul answered, "my prayer to God is that you and all the rest of you who are listening to me today might become what I am—except, of course, for these chains!"

[30]Then the King, the Governor, Bernice, and all the others got up, [31]and after leaving they said to each other, "This man has not done anything for which he should die or be put in prison." [32]And Agrippa said to Festus, "This man could have been released if he had not appealed to the Emperor."

## Paul Sails for Rome

27 When it was decided that we should sail to Italy, they handed Paul and some other prisoners over to Julius, an officer in the Roman army regiment called "The Emperor's Regiment." [2]We went aboard a ship from Adramyttium, which was ready to leave for the seaports of the province of Asia, and sailed away. Aristarchus, a Macedonian from Thessalonica, was with us. [3]The next day we arrived at Sidon. Julius was kind to Paul and allowed him to go and see his friends, to be

given what he needed. ⁴We went on from there, and because the winds were blowing against us we sailed on the sheltered side of the island of Cyprus. ⁵We crossed over the sea off Cilicia and Pamphylia, and came to Myra, in Lycia. ⁶There the officer found a ship from Alexandria that was going to sail for Italy, so he put us aboard.

⁷We sailed slowly for several days, and with great difficulty finally arrived off the town of Cnidus. The wind would not let us go any farther in that direction, so we sailed down the sheltered side of the island of Crete, passing by Cape Salmone. ⁸We kept close to the coast, and with great difficulty came to a place called Safe Harbors, not far from the town of Lasea.

⁹We spent a long time there, until it became dangerous to continue the voyage, because by now the day of Atonement was already past. So Paul gave them this advice, ¹⁰"Men, I see that our voyage from here on will be dangerous; there will be great damage to the cargo and to the ship, and loss of life as well." ¹¹But the army officer was convinced by what the captain and the owner of the ship said, and not by what Paul said. ¹²The harbor was not a good one to spend the winter in; so most of the men were in favor of putting out to sea and trying to reach Phoenix, if possible. It is a harbor in Crete that faces southwest and northwest, and they could spend the winter there.

## The Storm at Sea

¹³A soft wind from the south began to blow, and the men thought that they could carry out their plan; so they pulled up the anchor and sailed as close as possible along the coast of Crete. ¹⁴But soon a very strong wind—the one called "Northeaster"—blew down from the island. ¹⁵It hit the ship, and since it was impossible to keep the ship headed into the wind, we gave up trying and let it be carried along by the wind. ¹⁶We got some shelter when we passed to the south of the little island of Cauda. There, with some difficulty, we managed to make the ship's boat secure. ¹⁷They pulled it aboard, and then fastened some ropes tight around the ship. They were afraid that they might run into the sandbanks off the

coast of Libya; so they lowered the sail and let the ship be carried by the wind. ¹⁸The violent storm continued, so on the next day they began to throw the ship's cargo overboard, ¹⁹and on the following day they threw the ship's equipment overboard with their own hands. ²⁰For many days we could not see the sun or the stars, and the wind kept on blowing very hard. We finally gave up all hope of being saved.

²¹After the men had gone a long time without food, Paul stood before them and said, "Men, you should have listened to me and not have sailed from Crete; then we would have avoided all this damage and loss. ²²But now I beg you, take courage! Not one of you will lose his life; only the ship will be lost. ²³For last night an angel of the God to whom I belong and whom I worship came to me ²⁴and said, 'Don't be afraid, Paul! You must stand before the Emperor; and God, in his goodness, has given you the lives of all those who are sailing with you.' ²⁵And so, men, take courage! For I trust in God that it will be just as I was told. ²⁶But we will be driven ashore on some island."

²⁷It was the fourteenth night, and we were being driven by the storm on the Mediterranean. About midnight the sailors suspected that we were getting close to land. ²⁸So they dropped a line with a weight tied to it and found that the water was one hundred and twenty feet deep; a little later they did the same and found that it was ninety feet deep. ²⁹They were afraid that our ship would go on the rocks, so they lowered four anchors from the back of the ship and prayed for daylight. ³⁰The sailors tried to escape from the ship; they lowered the boat into the water and pretended that they were going to put out some anchors from the front of the ship. ³¹But Paul said to the army officer and soldiers, "If these sailors don't stay on board, you cannot be saved." ³²So the soldiers cut the ropes that held the boat and let it go.

³³Day was about to come, and Paul begged them all to eat some food, "You have been waiting for fourteen days now, and all this time you have not eaten a thing. ³⁴I beg you, then, eat some food; you need it in order to survive. Not even a hair of your heads will be lost." ³⁵After saying this, Paul took some bread, gave thanks

to God before them all, broke it, and began to eat. ³⁶They took courage, and every one of them also ate some food. ³⁷There was a total of two hundred and seventy-six of us on board. ³⁸After everyone had eaten enough, they lightened the ship by throwing the wheat into the sea.

## The Shipwreck

³⁹When day came, the sailors did not recognize the coast, but they noticed a bay with a beach and decided that, if possible, they would run the ship aground there. ⁴⁰So they cut off the anchors and let them sink in the sea, and at the same time they untied the ropes that held the steering oars. Then they raised the sail at the front of the ship so that the wind would blow the ship forward, and headed for shore. ⁴¹But the ship hit a sandbank and went aground; the front part of the ship got stuck and could not move, while the back part was being broken to pieces by the violence of the waves.

*Holding on to the planks*

⁴²The soldiers made a plan to kill all the prisoners, so that none of them would swim ashore and escape. ⁴³But the army officer wanted to save Paul, so he stopped them from doing this. Instead, he ordered all the men who could swim to jump overboard first and swim ashore; ⁴⁴the rest were to follow, holding on to the planks or to some broken pieces of the ship. And this was how we all got safely ashore.

### In Malta

**28** When we were safely ashore, we learned that the island was called Malta. ²The natives there were very friendly to us. It had started to rain and was cold, so they built a fire and made us all welcome. ³Paul gathered up a bundle of sticks and was putting them on the fire when a snake came out, on account of the heat, and fastened itself to his hand. ⁴The natives saw the snake hanging on Paul's hand and said to one another, "This man must be a murderer, but Fate will not let him live, even though he escaped from the sea." ⁵But Paul shook the snake off into the fire without being harmed at all. ⁶They were waiting for him to swell up or suddenly fall down dead. But after waiting for a long time and not seeing anything unusual happening to him, they changed their minds and said, "He is a god!"

⁷Not far from that place were some fields that belonged to Publius, the chief of the island. He welcomed us kindly and for three days we were his guests. ⁸Publius' father was in bed, sick with fever and dysentery. Paul went into his room, prayed, placed his hands on him, and healed him. ⁹When this happened, all the other sick people on the island came and were healed. ¹⁰They gave us many gifts, and when we sailed they put on board what we needed for the voyage.

### From Malta to Rome

¹¹After three months we sailed away on a ship from Alexandria, called "The Twin Gods," which had spent the winter in the island. ¹²We arrived in the city of Syracuse and stayed there for three days. ¹³From there we sailed on and arrived in the city of Rhegium. The next day a wind began to blow from the south, and in two days we came to the town of Puteoli. ¹⁴We found some believers there who asked us to stay with them a week. And so we came to Rome. ¹⁵The brothers in Rome heard about us and came as far as Market of Appius and Three Inns to meet us. When Paul saw them, he thanked God and took courage.

## In Rome

<sup>16</sup>When we arrived in Rome, Paul was allowed to live by himself with a soldier guarding him.

<sup>17</sup>After three days Paul called the local Jewish leaders to a meeting. When they gathered, he said to them, "My brothers! Even though I did nothing against our people or the customs that we received from our ancestors, I was made a prisoner in Jerusalem and handed over to the Romans. <sup>18</sup>They questioned me and wanted to release me, because they found that I had done nothing for which I deserved to die. <sup>19</sup>But when the Jews opposed this, I was forced to appeal to the Emperor, even though I had no accusation to make against my own people. <sup>20</sup>That is why I asked to see you and talk with you; because I have this chain on me for the sake of him for whom the people of Israel hope."

<sup>21</sup>They said to him, "We have not received any letters from Judea about you, nor have any of our brothers come from there with any news, or to say anything bad about you. <sup>22</sup>But we would like to hear your ideas, because we know that everywhere people speak against this party that you belong to."

<sup>23</sup>So they set a date with Paul, and a larger number of them came that day to where Paul was staying. From morning till night he explained and gave them his message about the Kingdom of God. He tried to convince them about Jesus by quoting from the Law of Moses and the writings of the prophets. <sup>24</sup>Some of them were convinced by his words, but others would not believe. <sup>25</sup>So they left, disagreeing among themselves, after Paul had said this one thing, "How well the Holy Spirit spoke through the prophet Isaiah to your ancestors! <sup>26</sup>For he said,

'Go and say to this people:
You will listen and listen, but not understand;
    you will look and look, but not see.
<sup>27</sup> Because this people's minds are dull,
    they have stopped up their ears,
    and have closed their eyes.
Otherwise, their eyes would see,

their ears would hear,
their minds would understand,
and they would turn to me, says God,
and I would heal them.' "
[28] And Paul concluded, "You are to know, then, that God's message of salvation has been sent to the Gentiles. They will listen!" [[29] After Paul said this, the Jews left, arguing violently among themselves.]

[30] For two years Paul lived there in a place he rented for himself, and welcomed all who came to see him. [31] He preached about the Kingdom of God and taught about the Lord Jesus Christ, speaking with all boldness and freedom.

# MAPS

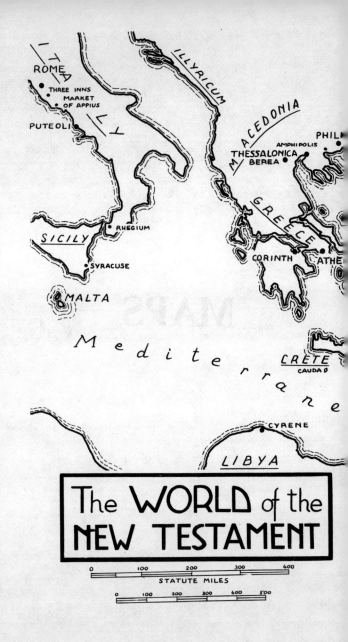

# The WORLD of the NEW TESTAMENT

STATUTE MILES

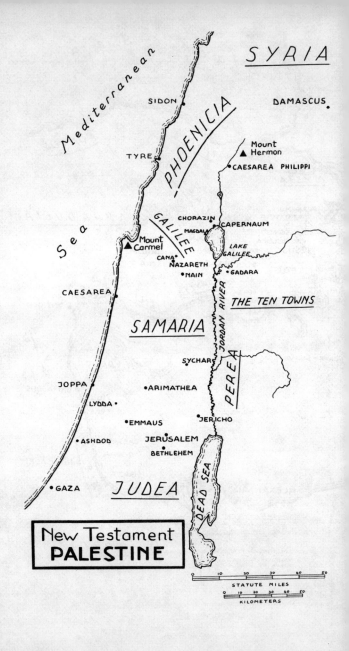

New Testament
**PALESTINE**

STATUTE MILES

KILOMETERS

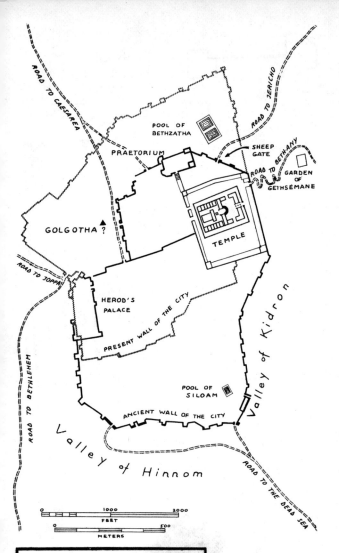

ROAD TO CAESAREA

ROAD TO JERICHO

POOL OF
BETHZATHA

PRAETORIUM

SHEEP
GATE

ROAD TO BETHANY

ROAD TO
GETHSEMANE

GARDEN
OF
GETHSEMANE

GOLGOTHA ?

TEMPLE

ROAD TO JOPPA!

HEROD'S
PALACE

PRESENT WALL OF THE CITY

Valley of Kidron

ROAD TO BETHLEHEM

POOL OF
SILOAM

ANCIENT WALL OF THE CITY

Valley of Hinnom

ROAD TO THE DEAD SEA

1000        2000
FEET
500
METERS

## JERUSALEM
and its surroundings

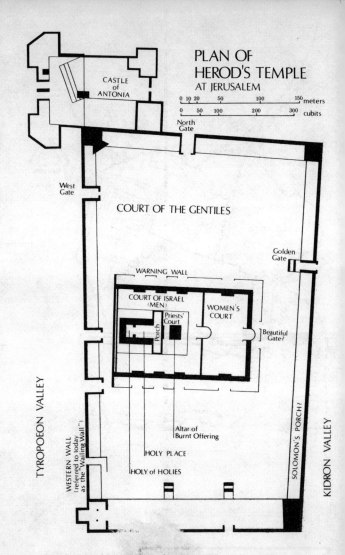

PLAN OF
HEROD'S TEMPLE
AT JERUSALEM

0 10 20    50         100           150 meters
0      50      100      200      300 cubits

CASTLE
of
ANTONIA

North
Gate

West
Gate

COURT OF THE GENTILES

Golden
Gate

WARNING WALL

COURT OF ISRAEL
(MEN)

WOMEN'S
COURT

Priests'
Court

Porch

Beautiful
Gate?

TYROPOEON VALLEY

WESTERN WALL
(referred to today
as the "Wailing Wall")

Altar of
Burnt Offering

HOLY PLACE

HOLY of HOLIES

SOLOMON'S PORCH?

KIDRON VALLEY